FRANK'S HOME

FRANK'S HOME

RICHARD NELSON

THEATRE COMMUNICATIONS GROUP
NEW YORK
2011

Frank's Home is published by Theatre Communications Group, Inc., 520 Eighth Avenue, 24th Floor, New York, NY 10018-4156

This publication is made possible in part with public funds from the New York State Council on the Arts, a State Agency.

TCG books are exclusively distributed to the book trade by Consortium Book Sales and Distribution.

LIBRARY OF CONGRESS CATALOGING-IN-PUBLICATION DATA
Nelson, Richard, 1950–
Frank's home / Richard Nelson.—1st ed.
p. cm.
ISBN 978-1-55936-381-5
I. Title.
PS3564.E4747F73   2011
812'.54—dc22   2011013340

Book design and composition by Lisa Govan
Cover design by Mark Melnick
Cover photograph: © Frank Lloyd Wright Foundation, Scottsdale, AZ / Art Resource, NY / Artists Rights Society, NY

First Edition, May 2011

FOR JOCELYN

PREFACE

What is a history play? I find it odd that one can go to the American theater and over time learn a great deal about the kings and queens of England, but almost nothing about our own country's history: where we come from, what our nation's aspirations, confusions, compromises have been. There are some illustrious examples of course to the contrary: Arthur Miller's *The Crucible*, Arthur Kopit's *Indians*, but they truly are rare animals among American drama.

When I submitted my play to Playwrights Horizons, the artistic director responded very positively, but also surprisingly when he said he liked it and wanted to produce it even though Playwrights Horizons did not really do historical plays. When I was talking to a friend involved in a New York play festival, I was surprised to hear her say that the festival accepted every sort of play except historical plays. I have since learned of other major theaters who will not even read what they call "period plays." What's the problem?

Mostly, I think there is a confusion about what is an historical play. There seems to be the misbegotten belief that the reason to write such a play is to dramatize interesting history. This is nonsense and has the whole thing the wrong way around. An historical play doesn't start out to dramatize interesting history; an historical play uses history to convey our own times. It's a method, a style, an approach to reflect things we as writers need to address and convey, about our world, our times, even ourselves. History can give us a critical distance that allows us to look more closely at ourselves.

Also, history allows a playwright to connect with our past, to not only draw parallels between different times, but to draw lines connecting them, and thereby show how societies are continuous and contiguous, how what we did affects what we are, and what we do will affect what we as a society will become. In other words, a history play places the playwright's concerns into a social context, even if that society is a hundred years ago.

A history play is always a way of dissecting large swaths of a society, drawing the parallels to large swaths of our own. An historical event or incident, we know, affects all of society, up and down its social orders; a depiction of this whole interrelated if not interdependent society is in fact an effort on the writer's part to organize society into some coherent organism.

I have written over the years a number of plays based on historical characters and historical events: *Columbus and the Discovery of Japan* about Columbus's voyage and what led up to it in 1492; *Two Shakespearean Actors* about the theatrical rivalry between the English actor, William Charles Macready and the American actor, Edwin Forrest, which culminated in the Astor Place Riot; and *The General from America* about Benedict Arnold and his treason. Each of these plays, I think, was an attempt to write about America, what it is founded upon, and an effort to rethink or question what we as a nation have become. *The General* was written as a direct response to the time of Newt Gingrich's Contract With America, when I was watching, I thought, my country reinvent itself into something it was never suppose to be. *Columbus* and *Two Shakespearean Actors* both center on not only America and American culture, but also on the role of art, or more particularly the role of the artist. This has been a theme that has continued to interest me a great deal. What is art's place in our society, what is its function; what is an American artist? In this way, I always saw the character of Columbus as a portrait of an artist—half visionary, half hustler—a man who sets himself off on an impossible mission and by chance, fate, luck comes across something else, something he didn't expect.

I had the idea to make a play about Frank Lloyd Wright or rather about two specific days in the life of Frank Lloyd Wright years before I sat down to write it. I suppose it took me all that time to discover what this story meant to me, why a fifty-five-year-old writer wanted to write a story about a fifty-five-year-old architect who looked at his country and found it confused, unable to respond to its inherent virtues and sense of self. An America that had lost its way.

Finally, I think pretty much every play I have written for twenty-five years could be entitled: "Home." *Frank's Home*, though, is the first where I've dared used that word in the title. It seemed appropriate, especially for a man who created beautiful houses, but perhaps no homes.

Richard Nelson
Rhinebeck, New York
April 2011

FRANK'S HOME

PRODUCTION HISTORY

Frank's Home was first produced in a co-production by Playwrights Horizons (Tim Sanford, Artistic Director; Leslie Marcus, Managing Director; William Russo, General Manager) and the Goodman Theatre (Robert Falls, Artistic Director; Roche Schulfer, Executive Director) on November 25, 2006, at the Goodman Theatre, and on January 13, 2007, at Playwrights Horizons. The director was Robert Falls; the set design was by Thomas Lynch, the costume design was by Susan Hilferty, the lighting design was by Michael Philippi, the original music and sound design were by Richard Woodbury; the stage managers were T. Paul Lynch and Jamie Wolfe (Goodman) and Barclay Stiff and Brandon Kahn (Playwrights). The cast was:

FRANK LLOYD WRIGHT	Peter Weller
LLOYD	Jay Whittaker
CATHERINE	Maggie Siff
KENNETH BAXTER	Chris Henry Coffey
WILLIAM	Jeremy Strong
MIRIAM NOEL	Mary Beth Fisher
LOUIS SULLIVAN	Harris Yulin
HELEN GIRVIN	Holley Fain

CHARACTERS

FRANK LLOYD WRIGHT, fifty-five
LLOYD, his son, thirty-three
CATHERINE, his daughter, twenty-nine
KENNETH BAXTER, Catherine's husband, thirty
WILLIAM, Wright's assistant, twenties
MIRIAM NOEL, Wright's mistress, fifty-three
LOUIS SULLIVAN, sixty-seven
HELEN GIRVIN, a schoolteacher, twenties

TIME

The play takes place over three days, beginning August 31, 1923.

PLACE

A hillside on the grounds of Olive Hill, Hollywood, California.

On the grounds are two (unseen) buildings designed by Frank Lloyd Wright for Miss Aline Barnsdall, a wealthy benefactress: the main building (Hollyhock House) and the guest quarters (Residence B). A third building, a schoolhouse, is under construction. It too is unseen.

From this hillside one can see the Pacific Ocean.

SCENE I

Outside.
  Olive Hill which overlooks Hollywood, California, and the ocean; August 31, 1923. Hollyhock House, a second residence, and the beginnings of a schoolhouse sit on the property, though all are out of view. Early evening, still a bit of light at the beginning of the scene. Frank Lloyd Wright (fifty-five) sits in a chair.
  A blanket is spread on the ground; remains of dinner— plates, glasses. Helen Girvin (twenties), a schoolteacher, and Catherine Wright Baxter (twenty-nine), Frank's daughter, sit on the blanket, picking at the remains of the meal.

FRANK: Sometimes—I think I am America.
CATHERINE: Father . . .
HELEN: What's wrong?
CATHERINE: I hate it when he talks like that.
FRANK *(Continuing his thought)*: Or what's left of it.

CATHERINE: Don't listen when he talks like that.

FRANK: She asked—

CATHERINE: She asked a simple, obvious, polite question.

FRANK *(The question)*: "Why have I moved here?"

CATHERINE *(Answering for him)*: Because he needs the work.

FRANK: Because this—here . . . maybe. It may still be possible here. Back home, they have all seemed to have lost their way. Chicago's bad, New York even worse. It's like they've just ripped up their roots. Forgotten who they were, who we are. They make money doing nothing now. Hard work—"for suckers." I've heard young people say this. And greed. And selfishness. What happened to everything we have been trying to do? They build buildings now that were in fashion in Europe eighty years ago. Or worse—in vogue in Athens—twenty-five-hundred years ago. They've forgotten how to look to themselves. Inside themselves— as Americans. You feel it getting worse and worse. In Chicago. Away for a few years, and I came back, I couldn't believe all that had changed. It wasn't where I wished to live anymore.

CATHERINE: And no one wanted to hire him, so he needs work.

FRANK: And no one wanted to hire me, so I need work.

(Smiling at Helen) California is young. I need youth.
(He nods to the attractive Helen, who blushes)

CATHERINE: Leave her alone.

(Helen "slaps" Catherine on the leg to tell her to "stop.")

Or do you like it? She likes it, Father.

FRANK: Not to make you any more self-conscious, my dear, but my God how I missed that—a young woman blushing.

CATHERINE: Father—

FRANK: In Japan, the women turn away, they cover their faces, but you realize they're thinking their own private thoughts. But an American woman's blush—you know her thoughts.

CATHERINE: Father.
HELEN: And what am I thinking?

(Helen looks at Frank, half smiling. Catherine is surprised by this boldness as they look at each other—flirting. Then:)

FRANK: But we weren't talking about me.
CATHERINE: When aren't we talking about—
FRANK: Helen was talking about the school.

(William Smith, twenties, Frank's assistant, has entered from the house and has started to pick up the plates.)

HELEN: We've based the school on the principle that nature—

(Catherine has been watching William pick up the remains of the meal. Frank has been watching her.)

FRANK *(To Helen)*: One second. My daughter has complained that I treat my assistants as servants. Is that how you feel, William? Like a servant?
CATHERINE: He's not going to tell you how—
FRANK: William? *(Then introduces)* Helen.
WILLIAM: We've met. I am whatever Mister Wright wishes me to be when he wishes me to be it.

(Frank laughs.)

FRANK: Was there an edge in that voice?
WILLIAM: Should I bring drinks?
FRANK: We're not drinking. None of us is drinking, are we?
CATHERINE *(After a hesitation)*: No.
FRANK *(To Helen)*: You were saying about the—

HELEN: Nature—our principle. Nature would have her children be children before they are men or women. The tragic error of our schools today is that we are so anxious for results of growth that we neglect the process of growth.

FRANK (*Referring back to his earlier comments*): My daughter has a lot of complaints about me. One reason it is nice to be here in California is because I have children here.

CATHERINE: And a grandchild.

FRANK: And a grandchild who will be coming to this school.

HELEN: I haven't met her yet. But tomorrow— I'm looking foward . . .

CATHERINE: I've been meaning to bring her by. So she wouldn't be frightened—

FRANK: You should have. (*To Helen*) I look forward to sitting her at my drafting table.

CATHERINE: Ann. (*To Frank*) You remember that, don't you? Her name? Ann.

FRANK: That's not fair.

HELEN (*Getting back on track*): We've articulated our goals—

FRANK (*Interrupting, to Catherine*): I remember my granddaughter's name, Catherine. I've been away. I'm sorry. (*To Helen, but speaking to Catherine*) My daughter has never forgiven me for—being away.

HELEN: It wasn't for—"being away."

FRANK (*Over this*): And so I've come to live in California— where she and my granddaughter are—Ann—to make up for this.

CATHERINE: Untrue. (*She smiles*)

(*He looks at her, then:*)

FRANK (*Trying to make a joke*): Not completely.

CATHERINE: Untrue.

(*They turn back to Helen.*)

HELEN: The goals? Of the school?

(Frank nods.)

To develop the child to the fullest. To encourage spontaneity. To free the child from self-consciousness. *(She has a brochure)* And the curriculum: English, Arithmetic, History.

(Frank takes the brochure from her. She continues, now at his side, on her knees, reading as he leans over.)

Geography, Drawing and Construction. Art. *(She looks into his eyes, then continues)* Music, Dancing.

(Frank smiles.)

What?

(He shakes his head, she continues to read.)

Physical Training and Games, French, Sewing, Civics, Cooking, Hygiene, Character Building, Dramatics.
CATHERINE: You don't have to read everything. He can read.

(Helen stops, but stays kneeling at Frank's side as he reads.)

FRANK: "The Little Dipper School." I hadn't realized that was its name. I've been labeling the plans—"the playroom." *(Handing back the brochure)* Very nice. *(To Catherine)* Another reason for being here—because there are people like her. She's blushing again. *(Smiling, teasing to Helen)*

What is it about young American women? I would just like to say that I am honored to have designed your schoolhouse, Miss Girvin. I'm only sorry it won't be ready in time for tomorrow.

HELEN: There's plenty of room in the main residence. We can wait. And for such a—perfect space. *(To Catherine)* I showed you the plans.

FRANK: I based it upon the children's playroom—when she *(Catherine)* and her brothers were growing up. I rebuilt that room four or five times.

CATHERINE: And then you left us.

(Pause. Helen, uncomfortable, starts to get up.)

FRANK: Sit. Sit, please. *(To Catherine)* And now—I've come back. To make this—home. And your school, Miss Girvin, is a good start. Start all over with the children, and do it right this time, isn't that the idea? Recognize our failures, and try again. Assuming our children will let us. *(Short pause)* I used to love working around the noise of children. I'm looking forward to that again. *(Looks back toward the house, then off toward the sea)* You know they offered me everything—in Japan, to stay. I could have built a city. They didn't want me to go.

CATHERINE: Lloyd said you were fired.

FRANK *(To "Helen")*: My son, Lloyd, is a very stupid man. Why my daughter listens to him I have no idea. They begged me, Helen. After what I built—the Imperial Hotel. I don't say this myself, but it's now been said—a new wonder of the world. They wanted more; I had to come home. But I'm sorry you can't see it. I'm sorry my daughter can't walk around it. It ate four years of my life.

CATHERINE: Lloyd said you were fired.

(Frank ignores her.)

HELEN: Maybe I will see it sometime. And I love this house— *(Points off)* you've made. Someone said it was— "Mayan"?

FRANK: Lloyd, her brother, oversaw the construction while I was in Japan, that's why it's so badly built. I feel the need to apologize to Miss Barnsdall every time I see her.

HELEN: It will be a lovely temporary home for our school. "Mayan"—we'll have to study that civilization.

(Pause. No one knows what to say. Then:)

Such a lovely spot up here. You can see the ocean. The whole city. *(To Catherine)* With your father now working here, it must be nice to have this to come to.

CATHERINE: Actually, tonight's the most time I've spent with my father in—what? Maybe fifteen years.

(Short pause.)

FRANK: A grotesque exaggeration from a spoiled child.

CATHERINE: Maybe—sixteen years.

FRANK: Don't you listen? Miss Girvin, I want my children. My family. I've come for them.

CATHERINE: And Mother?

FRANK: She's in Chicago. Happy.

CATHERINE: And giving you a divorce.

FRANK: She is. Finally! After how many years? That woman is tougher than she looks.

CATHERINE *(To Helen)*: So now he can marry his girlfriend.

FRANK: And why would I do that? *(Pause)* I've come out here to begin again. *(To Helen)* She *(Catherine)* doesn't listen. Or look around. I've set up an office. I'm looking for clients. Mrs. Barnsdall has been very generous letting me stay here.

CATHERINE: You're building her school.

(He nods. What to say.)

FRANK *(To Helen)*: So your first day is tomorrow?

(Helen nods. Short pause.)

(To Catherine) And you're bringing my granddaughter.
CATHERINE: Yes.

(Nothing to say.)

FRANK: I look forward to that. *(Hears something off)* William?!
   Is that a car?
WILLIAM *(Off)*: They're back, Mister Wright!
FRANK *(Standing)*: They're back. *(Looks at his pocket watch)*
CATHERINE *(Standing)*: I better leave.
FRANK: No, no, no! You're my daughter. Please. Excuse me.
   (He goes off)
HELEN *(Waiting until he's gone)*: He's—thrilling, Catherine.
   To have a father like that . . . I hope I didn't talk too
   much. He was very polite to listen to me going on and on
   about the school. I hope I didn't make an idiot of myself.

*(Catherine doesn't respond, she looks at her, then off
toward where Frank left.)*

But he seemed interested. I shouldn't stay too long.
   Tomorrow's the big day. The children will be terribly
   excited. To say nothing about me. I have to say I love this
   house your father has built. Hollyhock House. *(She looks
   off to the house)*
CATHERINE *(Distracted)*: The roof leaks, that's what my
   brother says.
HELEN: Well it hasn't since I've been here. And the other
   house—where he is. He built that too? *(Points toward it)*

So everything. And now the school. To just sit down and
draw something and have it come to life.

CATHERINE: It's not as easy as he'd like you to believe. Lloyd
says—

*(Frank returns, leading the group of a frail Louis Sullivan,
sixty-seven; Miriam Noel, fifty-three; Lloyd, thirty-three;
and William.)*

FRANK *(Entering, guiding the others)*: Look who's dropped
by. *(He gestures toward Catherine)* I told you she'd come
when she heard you were here, Louie.

SULLIVAN: Catherine . . .

CATHERINE: Mister Sullivan.

SULLIVAN *(Holding her)*: So here is the reason why my friend
abandons us in windy Chicago.

CATHERINE: Me?? I don't think I'm the reason.

FRANK: My daughter can't say nice things about me yet.

CATHERINE: That's not true.

FRANK: Say something nice about me.

*(Put on the spot, Catherine is flustered, doesn't know
what to say. Short pause. Frank laughs.)*

MIRIAM: William get some chairs.

LLOYD: He's an assistant not a—

FRANK: Lloyd get some chairs.

(Lloyd hesitates.)

WILLIAM: I'll help.

(Lloyd follows William off, as:)

FRANK: Louie, do you want something to drink?

13

(Sullivan takes the only chair.)

SULLIVAN: Coffee.
FRANK *(Shouting to William)*: Coffee! Irish!

(Awkward pause.)

CATHERINE: So how was the beach? That's where you've
   been, isn't—?
FRANK *(To Miriam)*: Catherine's been here. Keeping me
   company. Isn't that nice? She happened to be visiting—
   (Gestures toward Helen)
HELEN: Helen Girvin. How do you do.
FRANK *(Introducing)*: Miriam. My friend . . . *(To Miriam)* She
   was visiting—
MIRIAM: So you said.
HELEN: I'm staying in the main residence. Hollyhock House.
FRANK: She's starting a progressive school.
HELEN: Right here on the grounds. A progressive—
FRANK: My granddaughter's going there. I asked them to
   dinner. We ate out here.
MIRIAM: How lovely.

(Sullivan, who has gotten up, stands looking off.)

SULLIVAN *(Pointing)*: That's my favorite thing so far. The
   beach was good, but . . .
HELEN *(Looking off to where Sullivan is pointing)*: What is
   that? I've been wondering.
FRANK: The Roman Coliseum. Made of plywood for one of
   DeMille's pictures a few years ago. Now they just let it
   rot.
SULLIVAN: Humility for all architects.
FRANK: Next to it, I think, is the Hanging Gardens of Babylon,
   or what's left of it.

MIRIAM *(To Helen)*: Good dinner?

HELEN: Yes.

FRANK: Here come the chairs!

(William and Lloyd carry in a few chairs.)

(To Lloyd as the chairs get set up) You spent all day at the beach?

LLOYD: We drove around.

FRANK: Let's face this way, toward the ocean.

HELEN: Toward Japan you mean?

FRANK: No, I didn't mean—

MIRIAM: We never liked Japan.

LLOYD *(To Catherine)*: It's good to see you here. You said you'd never come.

FRANK: Did she?

CATHERINE: I never said that. Why would I say that? He's our father. *(To Sullivan)* How long have you been here, Mister Sullivan, I don't think Father said?

FRANK: Four days, isn't it now?

SULLIVAN: I've seen everything. Though they could use a skyscraper or two.

(Polite laughter.)

I'm trying to find out who to talk to about that.

(William returns with coffee for Sullivan. As Sullivan takes out a flask:)

WILLIAM: It's already . . .

(Sullivan ignores this and pours. The others watch.)

SULLIVAN *(Pouring)*: Anyone else?

(No response, then:)

LLOYD *(Pointed)*: Miriam?
MIRIAM: No. Thank you.

(They are all seated now, either in chairs or on the ground.)

HELEN *(Starting to get up)*: Maybe I should—
CATHERINE: Please, without you there's no one to talk to.

(Helen hesitates, then sits back down.)

FRANK *(To Miriam)*: She's starting a school . . .
MIRIAM: You said. She's attractive.

(Pause.)

SULLIVAN: I did some sketches at the beach. *(To Lloyd)* I left
them in the car.

(Lloyd starts to get up.)

WILLIAM: I'll get them.

(Lloyd sits back down.)

FRANK *(To Lloyd)*: He wants you to get them.

*(This stops William. Lloyd gets up and goes off to the
car.)*

(To Helen) My son. *(Shakes his head)* He now works for
the pictures. He couldn't get a real design job.
CATHERINE: It's a good job.
FRANK: So he does things like—out of plywood. *(Gestures off)*

CATHERINE: It's a good job at Paramount Pictures.

FRANK: So you had a nice time at the beach.

MIRIAM: Very nice. *(Short pause)* How long are we going to sit out here?

CATHERINE: What time is it now? *(She looks at her watch)* It is getting late. *(She doesn't move)*

MIRIAM: I'm going to get a wrap, my shoulders are cold. Louis, are you comfortable out here?

SULLIVAN: I've got my coffee. I've got the plywood Roman Coliseum and the Hanging Gardens of Babylon.

MIRIAM: Is that really what that is?

SULLIVAN: I can squint and still see the ocean. I've got a Mayan-looking house behind me. Why would I want to be anywhere else.

MIRIAM: You're not chilled?

SULLIVAN: No.

MIRIAM: Anyone else . . . ? *(No response. She goes off)*

HELEN *(To Sullivan)*: You're from Chicago?

FRANK: Mister Sullivan is Chicago, Miss Girvin.

(Helen turns to Catherine.)

CATHERINE: I don't know what that means either.

SULLIVAN: I am from Chicago. And where are you from?

HELEN: Me? I'm . . . here.

FRANK *(To Catherine)*: When was the last time you and Miriam saw each other?

CATHERINE: We've never met.

FRANK: Ah. I didn't realize that. *(He did)*

CATHERINE: She's attractive. I love her sense of style. It's all her own.

(Lloyd returns with the sketchbook.)

Lloyd says she has problems with drink.

(This stops Lloyd for a second, then:)

LLOYD *(To Sullivan)*: I have your sketchbook. *(Gives it to Sullivan)*

CATHERINE *(To Lloyd)*: Mother's finally granting Father a divorce.

LLOYD: We knew this.

CATHERINE: Father was just talking about it.

FRANK: Is it the right time for this, Catherine?

(Miriam returns with her shawl.)

MIRIAM: Right time for what? *(No response. Puts on her shawl)* It's gotten very chilly out here, hasn't it?

CATHERINE *(Getting up)*: I should go. My husband's alone with Ann. It's right about now that she begins conning him for candy.

FRANK *(To Catherine)*: Children.

CATHERINE *(Shaking his hand)*: Mister Sullivan, it is very nice to see you again, even though I don't remember you at all. I think I was a baby. If there's anything my husband or I can do to make your visit to Los Angeles more enjoyable . . .

SULLIVAN: Thank you, dear.

CATHERINE: It's a beautiful place. And—for us—it's home. Lloyd. *(Kisses him on the cheek)* Patience. *(Goes up to Miriam)* How do you do? I'm Catherine. The daughter. *(Turns to Frank)* Father. *(No kiss)* Don't get up. I'll see you again tomorrow.

(Frank looks confused.)

With Ann. She's coming to Helen's school. It's the first day.

FRANK: Yes. That's right.
CATHERINE: Two days in a row—seeing my father. When's the
last time that happened? Good night.

(She goes.)

HELEN *(Starting to stand)*: I think I should be—
FRANK: No. It's early. Please.

(Helen sits down on the grass.)

MIRIAM: I think I'd like a drink. Anyone else? *(No response)*
Helen? It is Helen, isn't it?
HELEN: I don't drink.

(Miriam starts to go, stops.)

MIRIAM *(To Helen)*: Where are you living?
HELEN *(Points)*: Hollyhock House.
MIRIAM: Just there? *(She looks at Frank, then back to Helen)*
That close. Do you know that seconds after Miss Barnsdall
left for Europe, Frank was over there rearranging the
furniture? He likes his houses lived in in a certain way.
HELEN: I know. *(She smiles. After a look to Frank)* That's how
we met. I was asleep and I heard this noise—it was Mister
Wright moving a table.
MIRIAM: You were asleep?
HELEN *(Smiling)*: Yes, and I—
MIRIAM: Did you come out in your robe? Your nightgown?
HELEN: I'm sorry?
MIRIAM: Did you put on a robe or not? *(After a look at Frank)*
I'll get myself a drink.

(She goes. And the men suddenly relax.)

SULLIVAN *(As he sketches, to Frank)*: So Aline Barnsdall has gone to Europe? I hadn't realized that. I hadn't seen her—

(Frank nods.)

Is that a good thing? That she's gone? You're still building the school.

FRANK: She's a client.

SULLIVAN: So it is a good thing. *(We suddenly realize he is sketching Helen)* Don't move, dear. *(To Frank)* You know I knew her in Chicago. Aline.

FRANK: I didn't know that.

SULLIVAN *(To Helen)*: Do you mind, dear?

HELEN: No. No.

SULLIVAN: Before she moved here. *(To Lloyd)* You knew her, Lloyd. *(To Frank)* My hands don't shake when I draw. Isn't that extraordinary. Why is that?

LLOYD: I knew her.

FRANK *("To Helen")*: Lloyd was married to one of Aline's "set." In Chicago.

LLOYD: She was an actress.

FRANK: She was that. How long did it last—a week? *(Smiles to Helen)* What was her name—Kelly?

LLOYD: Kirah. Her stage name.

FRANK *(Big smile)*: Oh—her "stage name."

(He smiles and winks at Helen, who smiles back.)

SULLIVAN: Don't move, dear. *(To Frank)* Don't make her laugh.

FRANK *("To Helen")*: She had my poor son wrapped around her little finger. He knows nothing about women.

LLOYD: I didn't know anything about her. But I soon learned. *(Tries to laugh)*

SULLIVAN *(Drawing)*: At least we can laugh about it now.

FRANK *(To the men)*: Aline Barnsdall always had very attractive friends. *(To Helen)* Still does. *(He looks at Lloyd)*

SULLIVAN *(New subject)*: Miriam enjoyed the beach. She took off her shoes. I sat under an umbrella. But she seemed to like the sun. Lloyd was very good with her. *(Sketches; then)* Nice to see Catherine.

FRANK: Let me see. *(Looks at Sullivan's drawing)* Lloyd's a wonderful drawer. Better than both of us. *(Calls)* William! Bring us a couple of sketchbooks!

SULLIVAN *(To Lloyd)*: And you said your father can't compliment you.

FRANK *(Continuing his thought)*: Which makes it even worse that he can't get a job designing anything.

LLOYD: I work in the pictures.

FRANK: Anything real.

(Sullivan moves his chair to get a different angle of Helen. He starts another drawing.)

HELEN: May I see?

(They ignore her.)

SULLIVAN *(To Lloyd)*: Do you have a girlfriend out here?

LLOYD: No.

(Sullivan nods toward Helen. Lloyd nearly blushes; Frank pretends to ignore this. William comes out with sketchbooks. Frank takes them and hands one to Lloyd.)

FRANK: Thank you. How's Miriam? Don't answer that.

LLOYD: I don't want to *("draw")*—

FRANK: Draw. Show him how good you are. *(To Sullivan)* He apologizes for everything. Like his mother.

21

LLOYD: I wasn't apologizing—

FRANK: Take it.

(Lloyd takes the sketchbook. William picks up a few remaining things and heads off. For a moment they all look at Helen, then:)

SULLIVAN *(To Frank)*: I didn't know you drew people.

FRANK: I don't. I'm not good with people. I know that. I'm drawing a building. A home . . . *(He draws)*

LLOYD *(To his father, as he draws)*: In the car, Mister Sullivan was telling Miriam and me about his . . . friend. She was—how old? Maybe forty?

SULLIVAN: About.

FRANK: I met her. *(He draws)* A great—beauty, wasn't she, Louie? *(No response)* He never showed her off though. I met her just the once. I remember the hair—fire engine red. That reminds me, you know what Miss Barnsdall said to me before she left? She said: "I want my school to feel green, Mister Wright. Not look green—just feel that way." *(Shakes his head)* Clients. *(Back to the other subject)* Red hair. A milliner? That's what you said she was.

(Sullivan nods.)

What a shame she died.

SULLIVAN *(Drawing)*: She was supposed to take care of me. *(Starts a new sketch)* A beautiful girl. *(He begins to sketch the milliner from memory)*

(Frank is sketching his imaginary house. Lloyd turns and begins to sketch his father. No one is looking at Helen now.)

HELEN *(After a moment)*: Mind if I move?

(No one is even listening to her. She gets up, brushes off the grass from her skirt. This brushing gets Frank's attention. He stops for a moment and watches Helen.)

FRANK *(Watching Helen and drawing)*: In Tokyo, I set the doorknobs on the guest rooms of the hotel quite high. *(Glances up at Helen)* So those small Japanese maids had to stand on their tiptoes, Louie, to reach them. I like the look of that.

LLOYD *(Sketching)*: That's funny.

FRANK *(To Lloyd, noticing)*: Why are you drawing me?

(Helen is standing.)

Let Miss Girvin have a seat.

HELEN: I don't need—

FRANK: Lloyd.

HELEN: I was fine on the grass—

LLOYD *(Standing)*: Take the seat. Please, take it.

(Helen reluctantly takes his seat. Lloyd stands, still sketching his father, and soon sits on the ground.)

FRANK *(To Sullivan)*: Is that the milliner? Put more hair on her, people will think she's a boy.

(Pause. They sketch. Then:)

HELEN *(Blurts out)*: My brother—

(They look at her.)

Do you mind if I say something? Am I interrupting?

FRANK: No.

(Sullivan and Lloyd shake their heads.)

HELEN: My brother—is a writer. He writes for the pictures. *(She smiles, thinking about what she is about to say)* Sometimes, I can be talking to him, and it's like I'm suddenly not even there. His mind— Who knows? But I know he's thinking about some story he's writing. Artists . . .

FRANK *(Sketching)*: Are you sure that's what he's thinking about?

HELEN: That's what he says.

FRANK: Oh. Then that must be it then.

(He shows her his sketch.)

HELEN: Is that a house you're going to—?

FRANK: I don't know. *(He sets it down)* Another home. I find I do it compulsively. Draw homes. Some I turn into houses. So tell me, Hollywood, it's a nice place to live? *(Before she can answer)* It wasn't just being in Japan for these years, it's really the feeling that there is no place I call home. Or can. Which, given what I do, is a bit ironic, isn't it? *(Really speaking to Lloyd, but "through" Helen)* My son here doesn't understand. He hears only my criticism—which I mean as . . . My oldest children are here. My grandchild. The sons of bitches building their conservative marble monuments have yet to find their way out here.

SULLIVAN *(Drawing; under his breath)*: Here, here.

FRANK: There comes a time when one needs or whatever to put one's life's pieces back together. I'm thinking this is the place. Which is why I asked, Helen.

HELEN: I like it.

FRANK: Good. *(He smiles, leans and pats her knee)* Lloyd thinks I'm just passing through. Another job. Catherine,

I think now gets it. *(Short pause. Stands and looks out)* It feels like a home.

LLOYD: And Miriam?

FRANK: What about her, Lloyd?

LLOYD: Helen, do you think she's going to like it out here?

HELEN: I don't know her well enough to—

LLOYD: She doesn't seem—to belong here. You can just tell with some people. California's not the place for them. But what do I know. What do you think, Father?

FRANK: You and Louie spent the whole day with her. How did she seem?

SULLIVAN: She seemed fine. Just fine.

FRANK *(To Helen)*: She seemed fine.

HELEN: So maybe she'll like it. *(Feeling awkward)* I must go. And finish my preparations for tomorrow. I've taught before of course, but— To have the whole responsibility. And the—newness. It's exciting but it's also—

FRANK: A little scary.

HELEN: Yes. It is. Thank you for . . . Good night.

(She heads off; Frank watches Lloyd watching her. William enters.)

FRANK *(To Lloyd)*: Like her?

LLOYD: What???

FRANK: Never mind. *(To Sullivan)* She's short like the Japanese, so those doorknobs . . . *(He smiles)* I'd like to see that.

(William is standing next to him.)

What, William?

(William whispers to Frank. He stands.)

Is she in her bedroom? You have the key?

(William hands Frank a key.)

SULLIVAN: Is there anything I can—?
FRANK: No, Louie, Thank you. Relax. Enjoy the view, and what's left of the light.

(He hurries off, William follows. Pause.)

LLOYD: Miriam—you think something's wrong?
SULLIVAN: What are you asking, Lloyd?
LLOYD: I hardly know her. You've known her—
SULLIVAN: She and your father have been together a long time. I've known her a long time.
LLOYD: Today was the longest I'd ever spent with her.
SULLIVAN: And she was on her best behavior.

(Short pause.)

LLOYD: She seemed pleasant.
SULLIVAN: She knows what's coming.
LLOYD: What's coming?
SULLIVAN: I think we all know, Lloyd. Don't be cute. He's not going to marry her. Now that he could, he won't. He told me when I got here, but anyone could see it on his face. Don't tell me this is a surprise.
LLOYD: I mentioned this "thought" to my sister, she didn't believe me.
SULLIVAN: So she came to see for herself.

(Lloyd nods.)

LLOYD: My god . . . *(Short pause)* To be honest what I had heard about her—I expected much much . . . Just different.

SULLIVAN: Miriam Noel can be very charming, Lloyd. Your father isn't a complete fool when it comes to women. Sorry, your mother excluded. Her—he should have stayed with.

LLOYD *(Distracted)*: My god . . . *(Getting up)* I suppose I should go home. *(Then)* Need anything?

(Sullivan shakes his head.)

Well . . . What's to say?

SULLIVAN *(Stopping him)*: Lloyd—has your father told you why I'm here?

LLOYD: What do you mean?

SULLIVAN: I've been here three days and he hasn't once talked about any work for me. He brought me out here to work, didn't he? Why else am I here? I can still work.

LLOYD: Of course you can, Mister Sullivan—

SULLIVAN: He knows that?!

LLOYD: Yes. Of course.

SULLIVAN *(Over this)*: My hands don't shake when I—

LLOYD: I saw. We saw that. I'll talk to him. If that's what you'd like. Or—why don't you just . . . *(Looks at Sullivan)* Good night. *(He goes)*

(Sullivan takes out the flask and pours, looks off. William comes in to retrieve the chairs.)

WILLIAM *(Explaining himself)*: I'm—taking the chairs back inside.

SULLIVAN: This one. Leave this one. *(The one he is sitting in)*

WILLIAM: Of course, I wouldn't . . . *(He picks up two chairs)*

SULLIVAN: William?

(William stops.)

Why are you here?

WILLIAM: Why am I—? To learn everything I can from Mister Wright. I wish to be an architect.

SULLIVAN: And so you learn by bringing drinks, dragging chairs out, then back in— Do you know who I am?

WILLIAM: Of course. Who doesn't know who you are, Mister Sullivan?

(Off, from the smaller house, sounds of an argument between Frank and Miriam: shouts, screams.

Sullivan and William pretend to ignore it. William decides not to take the chairs in right now and sets them down.)

SULLIVAN: And has Mister Wright told you why I'm here?

WILLIAM: I don't understand.

SULLIVAN: What projects he's hoping to convince me to work on?

WILLIAM: He hasn't.

SULLIVAN *(Continuing)*: As his partner.

WILLIAM: No, I'm sorry. What sort of projects?

SULLIVAN: Where are you from?

WILLIAM: Wisconsin.

(The argument continues.)

SULLIVAN *(To say something)*: Lovely view at night.

WILLIAM: It is.

(Lloyd reappears.)

SULLIVAN: I thought you'd left.

LLOYD: I had to use the bathroom.

SULLIVAN: Were you spying?

LLOYD: I wasn't. I wasn't.

(The argument off is over.)

William, see what's going on. See if there's something you can do, William.

(William hurries off.)

I wasn't spying. The things they were saying to each other. He hates her.

SULLIVAN: They've stopped.

LLOYD *(Looking off)*: I don't see anything. Someone's coming— it's William.

WILLIAM *(Hurrying back)*: Miss Noel is leaving in her car. I almost walked into her.

LLOYD: She is a sick woman. The things she said.

WILLIAM: I tried to get out of her way. She swung at me—

LLOYD: Where's Father? Is he all right?—

WILLIAM *(Over this)*: She's in no condition to drive—

LLOYD: Then maybe she'll drive off a cliff!

(Frank appears out of the dark.)

FRANK: Lloyd? Are you still here?

LLOYD: I'm just leaving, Father.

FRANK: The three of you just standing out here in the dark?

WILLIAM *(Picking up two chairs)*: I was bringing in the chairs.
    (He goes off with the chairs)

LLOYD: I'll drop by tomorrow, Father. Good night.

(He hurries off.)

FRANK: He heard that?

(Sullivan nods.)

He can't wait to telephone his sister.

SULLIVAN: No. He can't wait.

(Frank looks off, then:)

FRANK: She seriously thought we were going to get married now. *(Shakes his head in disbelief)* Because of the divorce? . . .

(Sullivan nods.)

What the hell did she think I came to California for?! What does she think I mean when I say I'm starting over again?!

SULLIVAN: She knew. She knew. She just couldn't believe— I don't know.

FRANK: I hinted. I hinted and hinted and hinted. I more than hinted, Louie. I finally just had to say: "I can't even stand looking at you!" *(Short pause)* I hurt her. I'm sorry. But what could I do? "Get away from me! I don't want you anymore!" *(Pause)* If we look too closely at ourselves for too long . . . It hasn't been easy. Months ago, in a restaurant I started to cry; I don't know why. Then I started to shake like I had a fever, but I didn't. Then I was sitting at the drafting table, and in the blink of an eye seven hours passed. My Japanese assistant said my face looked like a skull. I then lost my voice, or rather it became this slow, raspy old man's voice. *(Turns to Sullivan)* In Japan, the homes, there's almost nothing to them. Just—what is needed. And they are so beautiful. You feel they are— necessary. I need to strip things away. And tonight that's what I've done. What I've just done. And I need, Louie, to come home—or find one.

(Sullivan holds out the flask, Frank shakes his head.)

Why are we out here in the dark? Don't you want to go to bed?

SULLIVAN: You know I don't sleep.

FRANK: Come on, let's sit inside then. We can be alone in there. *(Looking off)* The lights are still on in Hollyhock House. That skinny schoolteacher's still up. She's— excited, she said.

SULLIVAN: Frank.

FRANK: Don't worry. I won't. Not tonight. *(Still looking off)* "Hollyhock House." What a stupid name. They don't let me choose the names. *(Turns back to Sullivan)* Miriam locked herself in the bathroom. She locks herself in when— It's not just the morphine now, it's—I don't know. I can't keep up. Booze and everything else. You have no idea how I've been living. I needed to do this. I'd waited too long.

(Sullivan starts to take in his chair.)

William can do that. Could you hear any of . . . ? *("the argument")* Anything—said?

(Sullivan shakes his head no.)

Good.

(As they head off:)

I start again. And god is that exciting.

SULLIVAN: Anything I can help with—you ask. I can still work you know.

FRANK: Let me help you.

SULLIVAN: I don't need help.

FRANK *(Stops, looks off)*: They pushed me to the edge of the sea, Louie. To here. And so here I must make my stand. Stripped down to just the essentials. To my fighting weight.

(They head off.)

SULLIVAN: So let's fight.
FRANK: I can do great things here. Great things.
SULLIVAN: We can.

(As they exit into the dark:)

FRANK: Watch your step. Lloyd did the landscaping—and he made a mess of it.

(They are gone.)

SCENE 2A

The next morning.
    Another part of Olive Hill: the patio/terrace of Residence
B. The residence remains unseen, off. From the direction of
Hollyhock House, off, temporary home to the new school,
the sounds of children playing, laughing, screaming. It is the
opening day of the new school.
    Table, chairs, maybe benches. Sullivan sits reading the
newspaper, as Lloyd and William enter with breakfast trays.

LLOYD: There won't be anything in the paper yet.

SULLIVAN: There isn't.

LLOYD *(Quoting an imaginary headline)*: "Wright's Imperial
    Hotel withstands massive earthquake."

WILLIAM: He can't get through—

LLOYD: Can't you just hear my father? That "gloat" in his
    voice. That self-admiration. As if things weren't hard
    enough for us.

SULLIVAN: You mean for you.

WILLIAM: Mister Wright can't get through to anyone in Tokyo.

LLOYD *(To Sullivan)*: He's so—damn lucky! He builds an earthquake-proof hotel and then the gods give him an earthquake to prove the point.

SULLIVAN: They have earthquakes in Japan all the time.

WILLIAM: No one Mister Wright speaks to knows any more than he does. Except that it might be bigger than first thought.

SULLIVAN *(Pointing off)*: Catherine's here. With her daughter, for the start of school? *(To William, who has put a tray in front of him)* I tell you every morning, William, I don't eat breakfast. I don't eat period. *(Short pause. To Lloyd)* You didn't go to Japan with your father? He never brought you over—to work with him?

LLOYD: No. No, he didn't.

SULLIVAN: William?

WILLIAM: No.

SULLIVAN: I wanted to go. I offered. Of course I was busy, but I could have found the time. I asked him the other day why he didn't want me. He said he never got that letter.

LLOYD: Oh.

SULLIVAN: And I believe him. Why wouldn't he want my help?

(Short pause.)

LLOYD: I don't know. *(To William, as Lloyd begins eating his breakfast)* Is Father still taking the whole day off?

WILLIAM: He's asked me to organize a picnic lunch, so . . .

SULLIVAN: Another picnic. I didn't come here for picnics.

WILLIAM: He wants to look at houses.

SULLIVAN *(To Lloyd)*: Don't you eat breakfast at your own home.

LLOYD *(As he eats, to Sullivan)*: You've seen the photographs of Father's hotel in Japan?

SULLIVAN: I saw the plans. I wrote about it.

WILLIAM: A brilliant piece—

LLOYD: That's right, I read that, too. A lot of—praise. Just— praise. So unlike you. And still Father didn't give you a job.

SULLIVAN: I didn't write that to get a job. I don't do that for a job. I give praise when it's deserved.

(Miriam appears, wearing the same clothes as the night before, though now she is quite disheveled. Short pause as they look at her.)

I didn't hear you drive up. *(To the others)* Did you?

MIRIAM: There seem to be lots of automobiles—

LLOYD *(Explaining to the others)*: The school.

MIRIAM: I didn't mean to interrupt . . . *(She makes a move toward Residence B)*

SULLIVAN: I wouldn't. I'd wait, Miriam.

(The others look at her, then:)

MIRIAM: Could I go inside and get a glass of water?

(Lloyd takes the glass of water off his tray, hands it to William to give to Miriam.)

(Looking at the glass) What is this?

LLOYD: You asked for a glass of water.

MIRIAM: I asked to go inside and get a glass of water.

WILLIAM: Here it is.

(She hesitates, looks at the others, then takes it, sips. She starts to hand it back to William, who flinches.)

MIRIAM: What are you doing? You think I'm going to hit you? Why would I do that?

(He takes the glass. As he does, she suddenly hits him across the head, spilling water all over him.)

SULLIVAN *(Standing)*: Miriam!

WILLIAM: I'm all right.

MIRIAM *(Over this, to William)*: Tell him I'm out here! He'd want to know that I'm out here! Let me just talk to—

WILLIAM *(Stopping her)*: I can't. I'm sorry.

LLOYD *(Nearly yells)*: Stay here!!

SULLIVAN *(To Lloyd, under his breath)*: Easy. Easy.

(Miriam looks at all of them.)

WILLIAM: I can't. He doesn't want you in there.

MIRIAM: He's told you that? He said that? *(No response. To William)* You little bastard. You have no idea what he says about you, behind your back. What he really thinks of you. How he laughs at you. *(To the others about William)* Frank says he's got no talent at all—except for taking orders! *(Laughing)* He'd make a good waiter! Or bellhop!! *(Laughing, hoping that Lloyd and Sullivan will laugh, too. They don't. Suddenly serious)* Does Frank know I have nowhere to go? I have no friends out here.

LLOYD: Father says you have plenty of friends. That you're doing "things" with them all the time.

MIRIAM: I don't mean those kinds of friends. He told you that? If that's the reason for— I'll stop seeing them. Is that what this—? Louis?

SULLIVAN: I don't know what to say, Miriam. Sorry.

MIRIAM: It's his children, I know. Why does he listen to them. After all these years. You think he'd know better. *(Looks at Lloyd; to Sullivan)* Look at him. *(Disgusted)* My god.

SULLIVAN: Stop, please.

MIRIAM: And that daughter. What rock did she climb out from under? He can't stand her, you know. Where am I supposed to go? Has he thought of that?!

WILLIAM: Haven't you checked into a hotel?

MIRIAM: No.

WILLIAM: Mister Wright was called last night by a hotel to guarantee the cost of a room.

(Short pause. Catherine suddenly enters from the direction of Hollyhock House and the school. She stops when she sees Miriam.)

I'll talk to him. Tell him you're here. See what he wants. *(He goes)*

CATHERINE: Miss Noel? What are you doing here? *(To Lloyd)* I thought you said—

LLOYD: I did.

MIRIAM: What?? What did you say? *(To Sullivan)* What did he—?

CATHERINE *(Over this, pointedly to Lloyd and Sullivan)*: Ann's already made friends. At the school.

LLOYD: I'm not surprised. Good for my niece.

(Miriam looks off toward the sound of the children.)

CATHERINE: Is that coffee?

MIRIAM: Is he sleeping with that schoolteacher? That girl? He couldn't take his eyes off her last night. What does he think I am—blind? I know that type. I've been around that type all my life. So—let him take her to bed. I really don't care. Get it out of his system—

CATHERINE *(Trying to pretend that Miriam isn't there)*: It looks like quite a success already. She must have twenty or so students.

LLOYD: I hear them.

CATHERINE: Sounds like more.

SULLIVAN: They're children. *(He is pouring from his flask into his coffee)*

MIRIAM: Let me have a drink.

(Sullivan's flask is empty. He hesitates, then hands her his "coffee.")

LLOYD: Don't give her—

SULLIVAN: She's not going to do anything. Are you, Miriam?

(She takes the coffee, and immediately throws it into Lloyd's face.)

CATHERINE: Oh my god!

SULLIVAN *(Same time)*: It's not hot. It's not hot!

CATHERINE: She's crazy. *(To Lloyd)* Are you all right?

(Lloyd starts to wipe himself off. No one knows what to do. Then to say something:)

Ann cried when I . . . I thought I'd come here—instead of just driving away. In case. I can see them from here. Until they go inside.

(William comes out. He goes to Miriam. All watch. He takes her purse from her.)

MIRIAM: What are you doing? Give me that! *(She tries to grab her purse back. She hits him)* Give me that back!

WILLIAM *(Rummaging through her purse)*: Are these the keys to your automobile? Are these them?! *(No response. He takes them, and hands her back her purse)* Mister Wright has asked me to drive you to your hotel.

MIRIAM: No.

WILLIAM: I'll leave the automobile there, so you'll still have it, and take a taxicab back. I'll leave these *("the keys")* with the desk clerk, with instructions. Let's go. Come. Get some sleep.

MIRIAM: Don't look at me like that. All of you. What an awful place.

CATHERINE: Father doesn't think so, does he?

LLOYD: No. And if you come back here again—

SULLIVAN: Lloyd!

LLOYD: Father will stop paying for the hotel! But I'm sure he'll pay for a one-way train ticket anytime!

CATHERINE: I agree!

SULLIVAN *(Over this, to Miriam)*: Are you all right? Are you going to be sick?

(Short pause. She shakes her head no.)

MIRIAM *(Looking off toward Residence B)*: He's at the window.

(All turn and look off. Catherine smiles a big smile and waves wildly, trying to get her father to wave back.)

CATHERINE: Wave back! Wave back! *(As she waves and smiles; to Miriam, without looking at her)* Get out of here.

WILLIAM: Come on, Miriam. Come on. *(Trying to help her, ease her off)* Watch your step. Careful.

SULLIVAN *(To Miriam)*: Hold his arm.

(Miriam takes William's arm, and they go off.
Pause.
Catherine stops waving. Neither she nor Lloyd can believe what just happened; they breathe heavily.
Off, we hear the children playing.)

CATHERINE: I can't watch.

LLOYD *(Looking off)*: They're getting into her car. She's letting him. She's not resisting. *(Short pause)* They're going. *(Watches)*

(Sullivan gets up.)

SULLIVAN *(To himself, as he goes)*: Now I need more coffee. *(He takes his coffee cup with him and goes inside)*

(After another pause:)

LLOYD: That was incredible, what you said.

CATHERINE *(Confused)*: What did I say?

LLOYD: You told her to get out.

CATHERINE: I did? I don't remember. It happened so fast. It did happen, right?

(Lloyd nods.)

She is gone? And she's not coming back?

LLOYD: How could she, after that. Father didn't even come outside—

CATHERINE: I know, I know. I have to sit down. *(She sits)*

LLOYD: And he sent William to take her back . . . Did you see her face?

CATHERINE: Didn't she look pathetic? *(She stands up again)*

LLOYD: And drunk.

CATHERINE: You think?

LLOYD: And something. Those were the same clothes she wore yesterday.

CATHERINE *(Looking off at the houses)*: I love the houses that Father makes. I love everything he does. How does he think them up, Lloyd? Helen gave me a tour of Hollyhock House yesterday.

LLOYD: It leaks.

CATHERINE: Who cares? He creates—worlds. That's what I finally realized. You walk into Hollyhock House—I love that name—and you are taken some place special. Yesterday—I hadn't been in one of Father's . . . I don't know in how many years. But yesterday, walking through, I felt so jealous: why were strangers living in Father's homes and not us. But now—she's gone.

(She turns to Lloyd who is brushing his coffee-stained shirt.)

Are you all right?

LLOYD: It wasn't hot.

CATHERINE: It'll stain.

(Lloyd shrugs. Pause. Off, we hear the children play.)

I didn't chase her away. You weren't saying that?

LLOYD: No.

CATHERINE: It had to be Father. Otherwise—

LLOYD: She's not coming back, Catherine. Father doesn't want her back.

(Short pause. Off, we hear the children play.)

Maybe we should all do something today. Together. Celebrate.

CATHERINE: Don't you have to work?

LLOYD: I've taken the day off. We were going to drive around. Look at houses. You can come with us. Show him things. He's going to live here, Catherine.

CATHERINE: She's not coming back?

LLOYD: How can she? We could go back to the beach. He might like that. The three of us. When have we ever done that?

CATHERINE: We haven't.

LLOYD: I know.

CATHERINE *(Over this)*: Kenneth's going to come by at lunchtime.

LLOYD: He can come to the beach, too—

CATHERINE *(Over this)*: He only gets an hour off from the bank—

LLOYD: Then it'll be just us three.

(Short pause.)

CATHERINE *(Looking off at the houses)*: I wanted Kenneth to see these two houses for himself, so he'll know how to talk to the possible clients. *(She turns to Lloyd)* He says he knows some possible clients for Father. Through the bank, he knows them.

LLOYD: That's good news. You hadn't said—

CATHERINE: They're society people, here in Los Angeles. Father will like that, won't he? He'll recognize the type of person when he sees them. He'll understand that he'll have to behave himself, won't he? He can't just say anything.

LLOYD: I think Father can do that.

CATHERINE *(Another thought as her mind races)*: You know that Father and Kenneth have never met?

LLOYD: I know, I know.

CATHERINE *(Over this)*: Think of it: my husband and my father haven't met. What that woman has done to us, Lloyd. It makes me sick just to—

LLOYD: She's gone. She's gone, Catherine!

CATHERINE: Sh-sh! *(She suddenly turns toward the sound of the children)* I thought I heard Ann crying.

(She listens. Sullivan enters with his coffee.)

Sh-sh.

(Sullivan walks more quietly.)

No. That's not her. *(To Lloyd)* Kenneth was going to come with me this morning. But we thought that might be too much for Ann. Too much to separate from, I mean.

LLOYD: Sure.

CATHERINE: She's already made friends.

LLOYD: You said. *(He is wiping his shirt again)*

CATHERINE: Use the water.

(He takes a napkin and dips it into a glass of water, but before he can begin to clean, Catherine sings:)

> For I am a Pirate King!
> And it is, it is a glorious thing
> To be a Pirate King!

(She bursts out laughing.)

LLOYD: What are you doing?

CATHERINE: Don't you remember?

LLOYD: Of course I do. *(To Sullivan)* At holidays we'd sing—

CATHERINE: Father'd sing when we were children.

LLOYD: We'd have parties.

CATHERINE: Each year Father'd pick a different show—

LLOYD *(Sings)*:
> Oh, better far to live and die
> Under the brave black flag I fly . . .

CATHERINE: After Father left—

LLOYD: Mother would sing to us.

CATHERINE *(Sings)*:
> Than play a sanctimonious part,

CATHERINE AND LLOYD *(Sing)*:
   With a Pirate head and a Pirate heart . . .

(They stop, the emotion of the memory is hard to contain.)

CATHERINE *(Finally)*: Why don't you change that. *("his shirt")* I hate looking at it. Maybe Father—he probably has a shirt. I'll bet you'd like to wear one of his shirts.
LLOYD: I would. I really would. I'll go and find one.

(He stands to go.)

CATHERINE: And while you're in there, tell Father we're taking him away for the rest of the day! And not to look at houses! He's not allowed to do any work! And we won't take no for an answer. Don't tell him where. Let's surprise him.
LLOYD: And if he resists, I'll kidnap him.
CATHERINE *(Suddenly laughs)*: Just like we used to!
LLOYD: Just like we used to!
CATHERINE *(To Sullivan)*: I'd forgotten about that.
LLOYD *(Same time, to Sullivan)*: When we were kids we'd pretend to kidnap him, and make him eat lunch with us . . . *(To Catherine)* You remember that?
CATHERINE: I remember everything.

(Lloyd starts to go.)

SULLIVAN: He won't go.

(Lloyd stops.)

He can't.

LLOYD: What?

CATHERINE *(Same time)*: Why?

SULLIVAN: The earthquake in Tokyo. He just heard on the telephone. His hotel—collapsed . . .

SCENE 2B

The same. Around two P.M.
   Kenneth Baxter, thirty, in a business suit, with Catherine and Lloyd.

KENNETH: I can't stay.
CATHERINE *(To Lloyd)*: How long are they going to . . . ? *("talk")*

(They see Sullivan approaching from Residence B.)

   Is my father still in there with the reporter?
SULLIVAN *(Nods, then)*: I couldn't listen anymore. Buildings
   fall down every day. You'd think Frank had blown it up.
LLOYD: It probably doesn't help that he boasted to anyone
   who'd listen that—
CATHERINE: Lloyd—
LLOYD *(Over this)*: —"it can withstand any earthquake God
   can throw at it." The man was so damn arrogant.

CATHERINE: Lloyd. *(Short pause)* I feel for Father. *(Then)* Mister Sullivan, I don't think you've met my husband, Kenneth.

KENNETH: How do you do?

(They shake.)

SULLIVAN: How do you do? You're the banker.

KENNETH *(Nods, smiles)*: Everyone likes a banker.

SULLIVAN: I'm not sure if that's—

CATHERINE: Mister Sullivan is also an architect, Kenneth. Or was?

LLOYD: Is.

KENNETH *(To Catherine)*: I can't help him, too, Catherine—

CATHERINE: I wasn't saying . . . Sh-sh.

(Awkward pause.)

KENNETH: I should have been back at the office by . . . *(Looks at his watch)*

CATHERINE: Another minute. *(Looks at Lloyd)* Lloyd, you look pale. Are you all right?

(Sullivan pours from his flask into his coffee. Kenneth watches.)

KENNETH *(To Catherine, about the whiskey)*: It's two in the afternoon.

CATHERINE: Kenneth said he heard about it on the radio. The earthquake.

SULLIVAN *(To Kenneth)*: You look like you'd like a drink.

KENNETH: No. Thank you.

SULLIVAN: Anyone else?

LLOYD *(Over this)*: Did they mention Father's hotel?

KENNETH: No.

CATHERINE: So . . . And it's not his fault anyway. Is it, Lloyd?

LLOYD: I don't know.

SULLIVAN: That reporter says he's been told that the Imperial was one of the first buildings to collapse. Engulfed in flames, sparking fireballs which career across Tokyo. He asked your father if he thought anyone now would even hire him to design a chicken coop. *(Drinks)* That's when I left.

(Kenneth looks at Catherine.)

CATHERINE: One more minute.

KENNETH: I really have to—

CATHERINE: I know, I know. Oh here he comes!

(Frank enters, coming from the house.
They somberly greet him: "Father," "Frank." Then wait for him to say something.)

FRANK: What happened to lunch? I thought we were having lunch.

LLOYD: No one was hungry.

CATHERINE: I'll get you something from the—

FRANK *(Looking at Kenneth)*: Is this the . . . ?

CATHERINE: Kenneth. Father, this is Kenneth.

(They shake hands.)

FRANK: So we meet.

KENNETH: I'm embarrassed that it's taken us so long—

FRANK: How do you do.

KENNETH: I have to—

CATHERINE: Kenneth has to get back to the bank, Father.

FRANK: Nice to meet you.

KENNETH: I can stay for a few minutes more.

FRANK: Good for you.

(Short awkward pause.)

KENNETH: I am terribly sorry about . . .
FRANK: Should we sit down? Or don't you have that much
time?

(They sit.)

CATHERINE: I'll get another chair. *(She hurries off)*

(Another awkward moment, broken by:)

KENNETH: You have a wonderful daughter.
FRANK: Thank you.
KENNETH: It has been hard on her—not seeing you.
FRANK: She could have seen me.

(Lloyd turns away.)

What do you want to say, Lloyd?
KENNETH: I think you know what I mean, sir.

(Catherine returns with the chair, all smiles.)

FRANK *(To Sullivan)*: We've never met.
SULLIVAN: I know.
FRANK: Lloyd, if you have something to say . . .
CATHERINE: Father, Kenneth has some business to talk about
with you.
KENNETH *(To Catherine)*: Is this the right—?
CATHERINE: It's fine.
FRANK: What business?
CATHERINE: It's a surprise. Kenneth?

KENNETH *(To Catherine)*: I really don't know if this is—
CATHERINE: Please. Father's listening.

(Frank gestures: "Go ahead.")

KENNETH: I think Catherine has told you—I know some people, some potential "clients"—from the bank. They're interested in—building their dream houses. Whatever that means. *(Smiles, then)* I'd be happy to introduce you to them.
FRANK *(To Catherine)*: Is this the surprise?
KENNETH: They've heard of you.
FRANK: Have they?
KENNETH: I was surprised by that, too. I mentioned your name—I can set up meetings . . .

(Catherine smiles a big smile.)

Of course this Japan news won't help.

(Catherine stops smiling.)

(To Catherine) I had to say that.

(She nods.)

(To Frank) And you'll probably have to be a little more, what's the word—"flexible" than you may be used to. I'm not sure what that means, Catherine said I should say it. That you'd understand. *(No response)* One—potential client—a very nice couple—good income—family people—said: *(He smiles)* "I certainly wouldn't want anything—'Mayan.'" I didn't understand what they meant, then when I saw— *(Gestures toward Hollyhock House)* I told them I'm sure you'd listen to what they want. After all, they're the ones who are going to be living

in it. So—just as a little warning—for them—"Mayan" is not the way to head.

FRANK: Thank you. That's good to know.

(Another big smile from Catherine who is pleased with how this is going. Kenneth starts taking out photographs from a magazine; Catherine encourages him.)

KENNETH: Catherine had these photographs. I'd never seen them—of some of your houses in Chicago.

FRANK: Really?

CATHERINE: Mother sent them. They were in a magazine . . .

FRANK: Oh.

KENNETH: And—I hope you don't think this was too forward, but since the reaction was so—to the "Mayan"—well, I showed one possible client these, and he and his wife, they got very excited. This one in particular. *(Shows him which one)* They said they'd like something like this. But with a slanted roof, I think he said. I'm sure you'll want to talk to him and get his thoughts. Pick his brain. See what he wants. *(Points to the photograph)* That one. Something like it. It's nice.

(Catherine continues to be very pleased with this conversation.)

FRANK *(Looking at the other photographs)*: Not this one? *(Holds up a photograph)*

KENNETH: He didn't like it as much, I think.

FRANK: And not this one? *(Holds up another)*

KENNETH *(Shrugs, then)*: Everyone has their own tastes. But you know that.

(Frank holds up the photo of the house the couple liked and shows it to the others, especially to Sullivan.)

FRANK: This—is the one. So—when do we meet? Obviously these "clients" are busy people, but maybe they can fit me in sometime.

KENNETH *(Big smile)*: I can arrange that. Then you will meet with them? Good. Catherine wasn't so sure.

CATHERINE: Kenneth—

KENNETH: I said: the man is a professional. He needs work. He'll do what he has to do. I also have to warn you that each of these clients has heard the same thing about— *(Gestures off)* And there's another house in South Pasadena?

FRANK: The Millards' house. *(To Sullivan)* That's a house I want to show you. *(To Kenneth)* I wasn't here during most of its construction either. I was in Japan.

LLOYD: Building an indestructible hotel.

FRANK: That's right.

LLOYD: That has fallen down.

FRANK: Falling down happens. *(Then)* Lloyd helped on the Millard House. That explains the problems.

KENNETH: There's a question of contractors. They'd all insist on selecting their own. That was their biggest point, actually. They'd heard about—

FRANK: About what?

KENNETH: Costs. Escalating, I think. Problems. Heard stories. It's a small town, Los Angeles. Leaks, for one.

(Lloyd smiles to himself.)

I told them how seriously you take these concerns and you'd do everything to make sure such problems didn't occur with their houses.

FRANK: You told them that? Without ever having met me?

KENNETH: I felt I knew what you'd say. You're a responsible man wishing to do responsible work.

(Frank turns to Sullivan.)

FRANK: Mister Millard called me one day. Fit to be tied. You could feel the steam coming through the telephone. "There's a leak right over my desk! It's leaking on my desk!" You know what I said to Mister Millard? *(Turns to Kenneth)* Move the desk.

(Frank smiles, Sullivan tries not to. Kenneth looks to Catherine confused.)

LLOYD: I never thought that was funny. Leaking roofs aren't funny for the people who live under them. And they certainly aren't funny now. With a collapsed hotel in Tokyo, and god knows how many people dead. *(Pause)* But my father doesn't care about this. Look at him, is that a remorseful man?

FRANK: Lloyd was in charge of oversight; he was here while the Millard house was being built.

LLOYD: It wasn't the construction.

(William enters from Residence B.)

FRANK: What is it now, William. Another of my buildings has fallen down?

WILLIAM: Aline Barnsdall has stopped work on the school.

(William holds out a cable; Frank doesn't take it.)

FRANK: Why?

WILLIAM: That's all her cable says: "Stop work on school."

LLOYD: She's obviously heard about—

FRANK: At certain times, we find out who our friends are and who are our enemies.

LLOYD: He is always turning his clients into enemies.

KENNETH: Is that true? Why would you do that?

FRANK: I don't think I do that.

KENNETH: You know you can't do that here. These clients are customers of the bank. Good customers—

FRANK: I don't do that! Don't listen to my son. *(He takes the cable from William and reads:)* He's a bitter jealous little failure, who doesn't have the guts or talent to find a profession of his own, so he has hooked onto mine. He's like a leach. Or parasite. *(Folding up the cable)* And Aline Barnsdall is a fickle little woman with some cash. May she rot in hell.

(Short pause.)

CATHERINE: Lloyd has a very responsible job in the motion pictures.

(No response from anyone.)

FRANK *(To Lloyd)*: You're going to just sit there, Lloyd? And take it? You're not going to get up and storm out? You're not going to give me a punch? *(Smiles to himself, then shakes his head in disgust. To William)* So stop work on the school. Tell the men.

WILLIAM: They've been told. They got a cable, too. They're gone.

(No one has anything to say. Off, the children can be heard playing.)

CATHERINE: The children are back outside. They'll be through for the day soon.

FRANK: One by one we're abandoned.

LLOYD: Now you know how it feels.

CATHERINE: Lloyd!

KENNETH *(Standing)*: I should go. I'm really late. *(To Frank)* How nice to finally meet Catherine's father.

FRANK: I hope I'm everything you expected.

KENNETH: You are. So I will set up those appointments?

FRANK: Thank you.

KENNETH: It was all Catherine's idea, so maybe you should thank—

FRANK *(To Catherine)*: Thank you.

KENNETH *(Second thought)*: It might take a while, they are . . .

FRANK: Busy. I understand.

KENNETH: Lloyd. *(To Sullivan)* Sir. *(He goes)*

CATHERINE: I'll just walk him to the car.

(She hurries after her husband. Pause.)

LLOYD: Listen to those children. Imagine that they are screaming.

WILLIAM *(Disgusted with Lloyd)*: Jesus Christ. *(Goes inside)*

FRANK *(To Lloyd)*: Now even William doesn't like you. And he likes everyone. Poor boy.

(We hear the children playing, off.)

So, are you just going to sit there? *(To Sullivan)* My son has no pride, Louie. And that is one trait I can't abide.

SULLIVAN: Frank—

FRANK: Look at him. How can he just sit there? At least— walk away! It's what I'd do if I were him. Or—hit me! Come on, Son. *(Pretends to box)* Hit me. Come on.

(He gets up and gives Lloyd a couple of light hits on the shoulder. Lloyd doesn't react.)

Louie, remember me taking boxing lessons?

(He hits Lloyd again, a little harder.)

SULLIVAN: I remember, Frank.

FRANK *(Stops. Explains to Lloyd)*: I was an apprentice for . . .
(Gestures to Sullivan) Years younger than you are now,
but already— *(Another punch)* Well, Louie's favorite in
the office, wasn't I? Some of the older boys, they were
jealous of me, so . . . *(Shows off his boxing skills; shadow-
boxes)* They weren't going to stop. And I wasn't going to
just sit there and take it.

*(Frank stands in front of his son, arms out, begging to be
punched. He gives Lloyd a quick hit, then goes back and
sits.)*

(Explaining to Sullivan, about Lloyd) A wannabe artist,
Louie. In the circles of hell of art—that's about as low as
you get. You're there with all the pathetics. *("Smiles")*

LLOYD *(To Frank)*: And you? Where are you in hell?

FRANK: I'm up with the godly.

LLOYD: How can you feel like that today?

FRANK: I feel like that every day. *(Puts on a big "smile")* Don't
you wish you were me, Lloyd?

LLOYD *(Looking at his father)*: Have you no conscience?

FRANK: What do you want me to do, Lloyd? About the hotel?
What can I do about that now?

LLOYD: Apologize? Admit a mistake for once in your life?

FRANK: I've admitted many mistakes—

LLOYD: Bullshit!

FRANK: That hotel was beautiful. A work of art. Both inside
and outside. It lasted—well, as long as it lasted. That
doesn't take anything away from—

LLOYD: That is obscene!! It's a goddamn building for people
to live in, not some—sculpture!

FRANK: It was beautiful—

(Kenneth returns, followed by Catherine.)

SULLIVAN: Look who's back. The banker.

KENNETH: Mister Wright—

FRANK *(Correcting him)*: Frank.

KENNETH: What?

FRANK: Frank.

KENNETH: Frank, Catherine and I—

FRANK: Maybe "Mister Wright" is better for now.

KENNETH *(After a beat)*: Catherine and I were just talking at the car. *(He points)*

FRANK: I know where the driveway is. I put it there.

KENNETH: And we both agree that we need a new addition on our house. Nothing—grand. *(Looks to Catherine)*

CATHERINE: No. No.

KENNETH: But with Ann, we thought . . . I know it's not much.

CATHERINE: And you'd be doing us a favor, too.

FRANK: Too?

KENNETH: Nothing—expensive. Just a . . .

FRANK: I see. Thank you. Thank you both. Very much.

(Catherine and Kenneth are pleased with themselves. Frank takes out a little notebook.)

CATHERINE *(To Frank)*: I told you he'd be pleased. What are you doing? What's he doing? What's he drawing? *(Looking over her father's shoulder)*

FRANK: It's just . . . *(He has drawn a few quick lines, then rips out the page)*

CATHERINE *(Smiling)*: A little house?

FRANK: How's this? I'll send you my bill.

(Pause. Then Kenneth laughs—thinking it is a joke.)

KENNETH: That's very funny.

CATHERINE *(Laughs, taking the piece of paper)*: I'll treasure this.

FRANK: Good.

KENNETH: I should go. We can't pay much . . .

FRANK: I'll send you the bill for that.

(More laughter. They go.)

(To Lloyd) I will.

LLOYD: May be the only job you'll get for a while now.

FRANK: What Lloyd doesn't understand, Louie.

SULLIVAN: I'm not going to be in the middle. *(Gets up and goes)*

FRANK: He needs a drink.

LLOYD: What don't I understand, Father? I think I understand things very well.

FRANK: Then go ahead. Give it to me. Tell me what you know. I know you've been waiting for me to stumble. Now I have. Hit back. I've watched you always—judging me.

LLOYD *(Smiles incredulously)*: Me?

FRANK: I know you think I'm doing the same to you. But I'm really watching you look at me. What do you really know? I've lived a—complicated life. I have many enemies. You don't think I know how they'll attack this carcass of mine. One reporter was only the beginning. There'll be many, many more. You think I don't see the vultures circling? And this could not have come at a worse time for me. God I know that.

LLOYD: What about for those in Tokyo? Could it have come at a worse time for them?

FRANK: I feel terrible for them. Some of those people are my friends. My colleagues. I've tried desperately to get through. William keeps trying. I lived with these people, Lloyd. I'm heartbroken.

(Lloyd just smiles to himself and shakes his head.)

So don't believe me. *(Starts again)* I have been hoping to start again here. I've said all this. And this is still my intention. You say, Lloyd, that I do not admit mistakes. Well, here is a mistake I do admit—you.

(Lloyd looks at him.)

And your sister, to some extent. I blame me for what you are. What you don't know. But maybe, just maybe, I can make up for that—to you. To Catherine. Here. It was one reason I came here.

(Lloyd stares at his father.)

Now—where to begin. To make up for what you've missed. All you don't know that I could have— I could have taught you. Why not start now? Here—Lloyd—is what I know. Listen. And listen carefully. Especially now, because it's times like this, that what I'm about to say, we cannot be allowed to forget. *(Short pause)* Beauty, Lloyd. Beauty. How do we look at the world? Why is it we seek beauty? "The perception of beauty is a moral test." Thoreau said that. Beauty is not just a pleasure, an ornament, an—extra; it is not even a roof, or a door, or a floor. It is right and wrong. It is good and it is bad. The Imperial Hotel is—was—a quite beautiful building. I think. I tried my best.

And now—I have to believe that that was enough. For however long—

LLOYD: That's not how you talked about the hotel. What about those "miraculous floating foundations" making it "impervious to earthquakes, anything . . ."?

FRANK: I say a lot of things. To clients. To critics. *(Short pause)* What I argue and the art I create are maybe two different things. Have you thought about that? The hotel was beautiful. That is enough. So let me be proud of that accomplishment. A far greater accomplishment and more difficult than— What you see as failure? And disappointment? I see as the erosion say of time. Perfectly normal, expected, maybe in this case shorter than expected but we are not God. *(Making a joke)* Unfortunately.

LLOYD *(Ignoring the joke)*: I don't believe a word you say, and I'm not sure you do either. You're just looking for any justification to get you out of the mess you're in. Once again, you're trying to talk your way out.

FRANK: You're not listening. That's unfair.

LLOYD: You lie about everything. Ask Mother.

FRANK: That was a different sort of lie. I'm talking about art and beauty! Important things!! If you'd listen, Son, you just might learn something! *(Calms himself, then tries again to explain)* Look around at the houses here in California, Lloyd. Or back in Chicago. Look at what's being built today in this country. The vulgar, wicked, moral lies, extravagant waste, social, aesthetic excrement. To attempt to create a bit of beauty within this . . .

(As he searchs for the word, Sullivan returns with his coffee. He realizes that he is interrupting.)

Stay, Louie. Stay. There's nothing I'm going to say that Louis Sullivan didn't teach me. As I was saying: to attempt to create a bit of beauty within this— *(Searches for the word)* Catastrophe. *(He gestures across the landscape)* This country. That's what it's become now—a catastrophe. Which is why I find myself pushed now to here. To the edge. There is no further I can go, and still be in this country. Here—to find beauty, to make art. And that is so very important. That, Lloyd—is a moral act. It is a political act. A patriotic and religious act that far supersedes the survival of one building.

LLOYD: And the deaths of many people?!

FRANK *(Finally upset)*: My building did not cause their deaths!!

LLOYD *(Shouts back)*: It fell on them!

FRANK *(Over this)*: You're not listening, Son! A moral act! A political and patriotic and religious act! To find beauty in this mess—that's all there is. If you can understand one thing, understand this! And you will see why I can't let this stop me! Why I must not stop! *(Pause)* Beauty, Son— it's not just decoration, a painted face. It's our life and death. Our reason. Our meaning. And what we are—as human beings. *(Short pause)* Now tell me, what don't you understand?

LLOYD: I think you are a great artist, Father.

(They look at each other.)

A con artist.

FRANK: No, Lloyd. You're not listening.

LLOYD: And I think I must have known that for a long time, but just didn't want to admit it.

FRANK: That is not fair.

LLOYD: You've conned me. You con your clients. You conned our mother. Who knows, maybe you even con yourself, I don't know. But I'm not going to let you con me anymore. Do you have any idea what you did to us? How you hurt us?

FRANK: I wasn't talking about my personal life—

LLOYD: I am!!

(Catherine enters.)

CATHERINE: What's going on? What's happening?

FRANK *(Lloyd)*: There is so much more than that. This—
(Gestures, meaning this conversation between father and son) should be about more than that.

CATHERINE: Lloyd, what are you doing?

LLOYD: Talking to my father. Finally.

FRANK *(To Lloyd)*: I am so happy to talk about all of this with you. But, tell me—are you interested? Tell me—what can I teach you? What can I share? Ask me. About art. Beauty. What I'm trying with my life to do. Ask me, Lloyd. Ask me what I know.

(Lloyd looks at his father, hesitates, then:)

LLOYD: Do you have any idea what you did to our mother?!!

CATHERINE: Lloyd, stop it!

LLOYD *(Continuing)*: I was the oldest. I took care of her!

CATHERINE: This isn't the time! Stop!!

FRANK *(Half to himself)*: Say what you need to say, Son.

LLOYD: He talks about morality. I don't know how you live with yourself. What you must go through not to look at yourself. Hear the garbage that comes out of that mouth.

(Catherine grabs Lloyd's arm.)

CATHERINE: School's out. Ann's waiting for me. She can hear.

(All look off and see Ann. Short pause.)

LLOYD *(Bursts out, to Frank)*: I want to know if you're listening to me?!!

FRANK *(Quietly)*: I'm listening, but learning nothing I don't already know.

CATHERINE: Father, we have to go.

FRANK: Have you said what you wanted to say to me, Lloyd?

(Lloyd says nothing. Catherine goes to her father and kisses him on the cheek. Then trying to make a joke:)

CATHERINE: I'm going to save that little thing you drew, and frame it. And don't forget to send us a bill. *(She laughs)* Lloyd, why don't you come, too? *(She goes and takes his arm)* Ann and I will drive you home, so you don't have to take the streetcar.

FRANK: Nothing more to say, Lloyd?

(Pause. Nothing is said. Then:)

LLOYD *(To Catherine)*: Thank you. I'll take that ride.

(He strides off.)

FRANK: Good-bye, Lloyd!

(Short pause.)

CATHERINE: We'll take him home. He'll be fine. I'm sorry about the—hotel. Good-bye.

(Catherine goes. Pause.)

FRANK: Did he understand a thing I said?

SULLIVAN: No. *(As he sketches in his sketchbook)* I've never seen you take that much from anyone.

FRANK: He's my son. I was trying to teach him.

SULLIVAN: I'm glad I don't have children.

(Short pause.)

FRANK: Maybe we should just get the hell out of here, Louie. And give up on this country. They love me in Europe, you know. What if this isn't the place? What if—I'm wrong? They're more open to new things in Europe. It's funny because they've got the old things right around them. But that's probably why. They're not trying to re-create something, because it's already there. So the new—is the new. Not copies of something old. We've forgotten that here, Louie.

SULLIVAN: You could no more live in Europe than you could fly.

(Frank stands, looks off.)

FRANK: To have the Roman Coliseum—in plywood—rotting . . . I can't tell you how much comfort that gives me. *(Smiles)*

SULLIVAN: William was in there crying his eyes out. I gave him a drink. I told him if you want to be an architect, you have to drink.

FRANK: We're not all like you, Louie.

SULLIVAN: No. I know. I sent him to, bed. To rest. We're on our own now . . . *(Short pause)* If I can help in any way.

(Without looking at Sullivan, Frank shakes his head no.)

I did come here to help. I came to work. Why else am I here, Frank?

(Frank turns and looks at him.)

I've been here four days; it took me nearly three to get out here. I've been wondering why you sent for me.

FRANK: What??? I don't understand. *(Then answering)* You're my friend.

SULLIVAN: Why the hell can't you give me a job working with you?!

FRANK *(Trying to smile)*: The day Louis Sullivan needs to be "given" a job—by anyone—is the day that culture in this country is at an end. The day, Louie, when you and I clasp hands and look for a cliff. You don't need to be given anything.

SULLIVAN *(Suddenly erupts)*: I haven't been offered a job in—!

FRANK: Please not now. I can't—

SULLIVAN *(Over this)*: I have designed one goddamn pedestal for one stupid statue in front of one damn post office in a two-bit Illinois cracker town! That's been it, Frank! For six years! A little ornamentation.

FRANK *(Same time)*: I know. I know. We all go through unlucky—

SULLIVAN: My hands shake, but not when I draw!

FRANK: You've just been unlucky!

SULLIVAN: What's going to happen to me? What am I supposed to do? I write about you. I wrote glowingly of this hotel. I praise you. Now what? I need help!! Help me, Frank!!

(Frank starts to answer, then stops. Then:)

FRANK: Bringing you here was a nice thing. A good thing. You live in one room in a dirty hotel, and for months now you've been weeping over the loss of your little "red-haired milliner." What milliner, Louie, I met him. He was a very nice forty-year-old man you lived with. And I am very very sorry that you lost him. So I brought you here because I felt sorry for you. I pitied you. And I needed— someone to talk to. *(Pause)* And your hands do shake when you draw. I'm sorry you brought this up. This wasn't the time. *(He looks at Sullivan)* It's good we can be so honest with each other. Now I need a drink.

SULLIVAN: Thank you, Frank.

(Sullivan leaves. Frank picks up Sullivan's sketchbook, looks at a drawing, then sets it down.
Helen enters. She has paint on her face.)

FRANK: School's out.

HELEN: They're gone. Finally. *(Smiles, pushes the hair out of her eyes)* Packed up by their parents. I'm exhausted. I don't think I've caught my breath all day. They keep you running, that's for sure. I saw you over here, I just wanted to thank you for last night.

FRANK: Last night?

HELEN: Dinner? With—

FRANK: My pleasure. Sit down, sit.

HELEN: I can't. I need to change . . . *(She starts to go)*

FRANK: My first day at school—I think my mother said I cried and cried.

HELEN: We had a couple of criers. Your granddaughter though did very well.

FRANK: It was nice having them here. Hearing them play. What's that on your . . . ? *("face")*

(She touches her face.)

HELEN: We painted our faces. I thought I'd—

FRANK: What were you?

HELEN: A cat.

(He stares at her. She sees Sullivan's opened sketchbook, and looks at the sketch he was drawing.)

Yours?

FRANK: Mister Sullivan's.

HELEN: What's her name?

FRANK: I don't know. There's a little more. *(Gestures to her face; she wipes off the paint)* You are like a vision. *(She laughs)* Appearing suddenly.

    May I ask you something?

HELEN: Sure.

FRANK: May I ask you to have dinner with me tonight?

(She starts to speak. He stops her by putting his finger to his lips.)

I find you very attractive. And perhaps it's because of the children, when I look at you, I see—a good person. And a beautiful person.

(She tries to smile.)

I don't often say things this directly. But it's been a long day. I like looking at you. I like . . . *(Reaches for her hand)*
HELEN: I can't. I—don't want to. I'm sorry. And I'm tired. *(She starts to go, then stops, trying to make things better)* Yesterday, I said to your daughter, how wonderful it must be to have a father like you.

(She goes.
    Frank is alone.)

SCENE 3

Olive Hill, overlooking Hollywood, the same as Scene 1. Later that evening. Two chairs. Frank sits and waits; he holds a glass; lamps are lit. There is an empty cup on the other chair.
Sullivan enters with his newly filled flask and a small pile of letters/telegrams.

SULLIVAN: William's up. He said to give you these. *(Holds out the letters/telegrams)* He's stopped even opening them. I could just throw them out.

(Frank takes the pile and starts opening the letters. Sullivan pours more drink for both of them.)

I poured a little more for William—he said he can't sleep. I told him we didn't need anything. Do we need anything?

(Frank reads.)

I said we can fend for ourselves. More abuse? *(About the letters)*

(Frank opens another, then stops, leaving a couple unopened.)

Are we staying out here all night?

FRANK: I thought we were just getting started.

SULLIVAN: So—whose turn is it?

FRANK: Mine.

SULLIVAN: What did I just—?

FRANK: One of your skyscrapers. How you were lied to. And cheated. And how every third person in Chicago is a goddamn crook.

SULLIVAN: So—then it's your turn.

(Frank fiddles with the letters/telegrams, then sets them on the ground beside him.)

FRANK: So—here's a good one. Mrs. Alice Madison Millard.

SULLIVAN: The Millard house? The one you want to show me?

FRANK: In South Pasadena. That's that way. *(Points in the direction, then continues)* Mrs. Millard. From Chicago. I'd built her and her husband, George, their house there, and, maybe I was a little overly appreciative since they didn't hold this against me, and had actually lived in this house with some pleasure, I'm told. They now wanted another one—out here—well how often does that happen to an architect?

SULLIVAN: Not often.

FRANK: She was—slight, but a nice figure. I like her feet. I could have watched her open one of those doors in the Imperial Hotel. *(Smiles. Sips)* Now, this is a mistake. Ugly clients only: this should be a rule. But here she was—and did she want one of those Spanish sores you see everywhere around here? With all that Spanish-style garnish? No. *My client, which is why she was my client, wanted a flesh-and-blood home.* She wanted—architecture.

SULLIVAN *(Seriously)*: You should have run.

FRANK: I know. I know. I thought about that. But again they'd lived in one of my houses for fifteen years. With hardly a complaint. Except the usual. So I was, I suppose—blinded by this. *(Another sip, thinks, then)* Did I say that Mrs. Millard and her husband, George, had a mere ten thousand dollars for this house? Maybe another two grand—everyone lies about this—but maybe not them. Who knows? And the bankers out here are like bankers anywhere. Look at my son-in-law. Anyway, we settled on a very doable design—large living room, fireplace, balcony over it, which leads to the sleeping rooms. Nice size bedroom, dressing room, bath, guest rooms, and so forth, etc. The normal. And she had real standards. She wanted "good" floors. "Good" doorknobs. Everything about her house was going to be—"good." Maybe we could "squeeze out" a garage? she asked, with a big blue-eyed smile. Well—why not? Lovely, lovely feet. *(Short pause. Thinks, then)* Oh, she says, there's this most wonderful builder!

(On hearing this Sullivan pours himself and Frank a little more.)

He's built a real and I quote "thoroughbred house"— what does that mean? A friend of her's house, it turns out. We go and see it. Seems—fine. We meet the builder. Seems—fine. "Well, what do you think?" she asks me, then, eyes wide-open, sighs. "Well," I reply, then catch myself looking down at her sandaled feet, "a woman's intuition is something I value rather highly."

SULLIVAN: You don't—

FRANK: No.

SULLIVAN: I didn't think—

FRANK: But it made her happy. It made her blush. So just like that the contract's signed. He signs—with a flourish. With that look in his eye of someone hungry to sign his name to—well anything. A contract? Or say the back of my shirt? Anyway, he begins. And, to be fair, he begins—just fine.

SULLIVAN: Don't they all.

FRANK: And so we trust him. Probably the last person Alice Madison Millard will ever trust in her life. That includes me. Especially me. And with good reason. Meanwhile, we turn our backs on the boring, shadeless piece of land that's been bought for this "home," and a nearby ravine has caught my imagination, where stand two very lovely, very elegant eucalyptus trees. *(As he sips)* Has anyone ever before thought of building in such a spot? I doubt it. People out here are stuck on setting their buildings on the top of every boring hill. A tic. Call it—a bad tic. Is what I think. We get the land for a song. Offer half of what they're asking, and they take it. Like that. *(Snaps his fingers)* This home, I tell her, will spring up out of that ravine: "framed between those two haunting eucalyptus trees." The neighbors love us, they're thrilled, it keeps their views open. *(Short pause)* The construction begins. In what seems like one minute, Mrs. Alice Millard has begun addressing our builder as one imagines one would an Olympian god. As the source of all information. The solver of all riddles. The font of all knowledge. I notice this with some concern. It's not a good signal for an architect to see his client suddenly hanging onto the contractor's every word.

SULLIVAN: No. No.

FRANK: Has she suddenly had doubts? I wonder. About me? Have her friends "gotten to her"? I'd been in the battle before.

SULLIVAN: Who hasn't?

FRANK: Why does it happen? Answer me that. And especially with the ladies. How quickly they fall for the first man who is quote unquote "practical." What does that mean?! He knows "pipe fittings," he knows "lumber," so he must know—what he's doing. For a woman a "practical" man must simply be irresistible.

(Sullivan nods.)

I bite my lip. I pretend not to see this. Anyway, what could I do about it? *(Sips)* Our handsome "practical" builder, by the way, has pulled in some of his "family" to help him with the . . . what? The work? The building? His lunch? Or maybe they are there to keep him company. Probably that. I'm not sure where he housed them. Or where they had come from. Mrs. Millard, by now, has "cajoled"— out of me about as much drawing and redrafting and time for overseeing the beginnings of the construction of her "home" as might have been spent on say your average good-size medieval cathedral.

(Sullivan smiles.)

I'm not joking. I'm needed back in Japan to add a few touches to my indestructible hotel, when she decides to leave for Italy for the summer, paying—in advance—our builder. No receipts asked for. She writes me in Tokyo that she has done this. She says she—"didn't want to compromise" the relationship by asking for receipts.

(Sullivan starts to say something.)

I'm just getting going, Louie. Lloyd, now in my employ, drives over every day to check on the progress. None. Mrs.

Millard comes home and finds—little done. Doubt begins to creep its nasty way into our triangle. And our builder? Where is he? Lloyd finally finds him—miles away—working on another house—one for himself. Imported marble floors. Expensive hardware. Oak trim. Huh. Odd. Lloyd digs a little deeper. And learns that everything, down to the doorknobs, is in his wife's name.

(Sullivan tries not to laugh, shakes his head.)

Don't laugh—yet. We've a long ways to go. The house now is maybe half built with a third of the money left. Where's it gone? Who knows—on imported marble floors? Oak trim? And then—surprise—our builder quits—no doubt because the money is drying up, though he says it's because of the tone of my letters delivered by Lloyd, and the questions I keep asking. Questions like: Why aren't you working?! How much is this costing?! When will you be done?! *(Short pause)* So what is Mrs. Millard, our heroine with the lovely feet, doing at this point in time? Well, she's writing, and I quote: "We are going to finish that building if it takes every cent I've got in the whole world or can get." I'm sure she was crying herself to sleep. But on one of my visits back, she puts up a tough front. She takes it upon herself to find new builders, one after another. I say no more. And they just keep fading away. To where? Where? Is there some special "community" where builders go to hide out? Finally, I get one. He's not any better, probably worse. And by now we're in trouble—with creditors, we have debts; we're now subject to ridicule, there's even a law suit—which I now learn, Los Angeles is a very fertile soil for. "Thank god!" I insanely tell myself, "I still have six thousand dollars of my own to put into this house!"

SULLIVAN: No.

(Frank nods his head.)

FRANK: It's the first builder who's suing—the handsome "practical" one? Who's built his wife a nice house? Just what he is suing about, or for, I never figure out—more oak trim? The judge, bless him, rules in our favor. Thank god, and that, finally was that. Wounds begin to heal, leaving—only ugly scars. Reflecting back, in one of those rare moments of quickly passing objectivity, I have thought that our first builder just couldn't help himself from dipping back just one more time into such a deep well of gullibility. *(Sips. Holds out his glass)*

SULLIVAN: More??

(Frank nods. Sullivan pours, as:)

FRANK: And so—up it goes! And this is always a very dangerous moment. When we dare allow ourselves a morsel of pride. And perhaps even the thought that it was all worth it, after all. And Mrs. Millard's money, or rather some of her money, was not wasted. We relax. Mistake. Have fun arranging the books and so forth, which Alice with her usual good taste has brought back from abroad. So there we are at the oak tea table, in the afternoon light, a roaring fire in the handsome fireplace. The inside, it's beautiful, everything we'd hoped it would be—as long as I don't look too close. Outside, our ravine's turned into an enchanting miniature garden. We've built a pool that catches the light. The eucalyptus and house compliment, complete each other, like frame and picture. So—we toast "our success." This unwanted plot in this old ravine— which we'd cleverly bought for a "song"—has been transformed into that flesh-and-blood home of our dreams, one full of grace and charm, much like, I raise my glass and say—like it's owner. *La Miniatura,* she names it.

I never get to pick the names. *La Miniatura*: beauty where
before there was only—nothing. *(Short pause)* But nothing
we do—escapes the jealous eyes of the gods. The Japanese,
they are aware of this and so leave on purpose obvious
mistakes in their work—as offerings to appease these
jealous gods. Our workers had done this as well—in
many, many spots. But Alice and I, apparently, had made
no such sacrifice. And so—comes the rain, a crack of
thunder, a downpour seemingly focused only upon our
humble ravine. A river, no one had seen for fifty years,
now carries street water and half the embankment down
the hill. And so it rises and rises, first through our
basement, until reaching the height of the dining room
floor. It seemed determined to float the whole house down
the hill. Mud everywhere. The basement. The first floor
terrace. Pilot lights went out, the gas heaters buried.
Books, even the fireplace wasn't spared. And Mrs. George
Madison Millard's spirit? No doubt as heavy and caked
with mud, as those lovely feet. And her faith, confidence
in me? What about that? I think it just blew out, with the
pilot lights. And my last sighting of her—streaks of brown
ooze across her face, head held in hands, those blue eyes,
seemingly blank—while she sobbed. *(Sips)* I know *this*
now: just because a place boasts "eternal sunshine,"
doesn't mean you still don't build a roof as tough as any
back in Chicago, where you build for ice and snow
and . . . The sun here, I now know, cooks these roofs month
after month after month until they are like burnt toast,
cracked and crumbly. And then for a few days—it rains.
Unfortunately, I didn't know that then. God only knows
how many leaking roofs there must be out here. No
wonder people seem so scared when it starts to rain—any
kind of rain, even a sprinkle. They must look upon rain
with unmitigated fear. Anyway, I now wished to make
amends, but Alice Millard refused all entreaties now,

insisting that others come and repair the floors, relight the pilot lights, scrape off the charming fireplace. Fix the roof, which of course was easy to do, as there was not going to be any rain for another year. And—we never speak again. My client and me. *(Looking off)* I have visited the house once since I've been here, kept my distance, and the motor running, just out of curiosity. I wanted to see if our house was still standing. It is, barely, I now suspect.

(Pause. His mind drifts, then with the story done, he turns back to Sullivan.)

Your turn. *(Before Sullivan can say anything)* I try, Louie. I try. A couple more drinks and I'll tell you about building the Imperial Hotel. Now that'll take all night. And more nights to come.

(Laughs to himself. Sullivan watches, listens.)

People think we control what we create. But we don't. I'm sorry my hotel collapsed. *(Then he shrugs. He looks off toward Hollyhock House)* Hollyhock House—it's already started to fall apart. *(Pause)* I'm broke. You know that?

(He looks at Sullivan who says nothing. Then:)

In Japan, one night I found I couldn't move. My voice went away—to some place outside of me. I could hear it at a distance. Talking to me. Nicely formed sentences. Making no sense. I sat on our bed immobile. Miriam was asleep, probably drunk. And I felt this—breeze, Louie. A very slight wind go by my cheeks. And I heard myself think—I have felt the wind from the wing of madness. *(Short pause)* I was designing the same furniture over and over again—for the per diem. I was spending more time buying and reselling Japanese prints than anything else. I enjoyed making the money, but . . . The wind of the wing of the monstrous shape of madness. Flying 'round and 'round me. In my bedroom. It took everything, all of my strength—to get up and come home. *(He looks at Sullivan)* When you let me visit you, instead of always coming to me, Louie, and I saw how you were living in one dirty room. You even owed rent on that. But you let me come and see—

SULLIVAN: That was my little milliner's idea, she—

FRANK: She wasn't a she, Louie. *(Short pause)* What was his name?

SULLIVAN *(After a brief pause)*: Samuel.

FRANK: Samuel.

SULLIVAN: Sammy. He knew he was ill and going to die. He wanted someone to see—what had happened to me. So, I suppose, they—you—might help. Sammy cared a great deal about me.

(Short pause.)

FRANK: So—as I was saying, when you let me visit you—I saw all that. *(Silence)* You don't want to take a turn?

(Sullivan shrugs. Frank begins to open the rest of the letters/telegrams. As he skims the letters; about Hollyhock House:)

I do think that house is beautiful. And that should be enough. That is all I meant to say to my son.

SULLIVAN: I know. I understand.

FRANK *(Still skimming the letters)*: We don't actually control anything. Buildings rise and fall; we do the best we can. Something—or someone else—decides the rest. I suppose we'll need to leave here. I should be able to sell a few Japanese prints, enough for our train fares back.

SULLIVAN: Back?

FRANK: Home? I suppose we can call it that. I know more people in Chicago than anywhere else. Why not? What do I have here? The three of us can go back together.

SULLIVAN: Three??

FRANK: I'm going to call Miriam. I think I'm making a mistake. *(He looks at Sullivan)* I can't be alone. *(Then)* She'll stop drinking. And all that.

SULLIVAN: She's a lovely woman. Graceful.

FRANK: And she will never leave me. No, that's not in her. *(Continues with his mail)* She'll take care of me. Like Sammy did for... *(Gestures to Sullivan. Pause. Skimming the mail)* I have designed a house for myself—set in the middle of a desert. Surrounded by walls. Inside—surprises. Worlds. It will never be built.

SULLIVAN: I've designed seven skyscrapers that haven't been built. I love each one like a son. Each more handsome than the next. I wouldn't trade them for anything.

FRANK *(Continuing to read)*: When I design now, I imagine not just the house, or the furniture, but I see the people and what they're doing. How they walk through the halls; where they sit and take off their shoes. I see them in pairs; though mostly I see them alone. Standing at a window, looking out at the night and the moon. Sitting in a chair, in the midst of a circle of yellow lamplight, reading a book with a red cover. In the kitchen, testing the soup. There is no sound. But they are there, living. *(He opens a telegram)* Imagining them, Louie, makes me happy. *(He reads the telegram to himself. His face changes expression)*

SULLIVAN: What? What is it?

FRANK: From the Japanese Embassy. *(He reads)* "Hotel stands undamaged, monument of your genius. Hundreds of homeless shelter there. Initial reports wrong."

(Pause.)

SCENE 4

The same. A few more chairs have been brought out.
The next morning. Off, the children can be heard playing.
Lloyd, Catherine, Kenneth, Sullivan and William stand, sit
in chairs or on the ground. Sullivan and William are reading
from a pile of newspapers that Catherine and Kenneth have
brought.

KENNETH: Someone in the office called at six this morning
and said he'd seen a photograph where it is the only
building left standing in all of Tokyo. Everything else . . .

LLOYD: I can't believe that's true.

CATHERINE: It says in one of those papers, I think the one you
have, Mister Sullivan, that something like ten embassies
have temporarily moved into Father's hotel. And with
now—a thousand refugees.

(Short pause.)

SULLIVAN *(Reading, and correcting)*: Twelve.

LLOYD: What??

SULLIVAN: Twelve embassies. Not ten.

KENNETH: I got two other calls from the bank. I don't know why they should congratulate me.

CATHERINE: Have you gotten calls, Lloyd?

LLOYD: Yes.

CATHERINE: To congratulate you?

(No response.)

WILLIAM *(Reading one of the papers)*: They quote a Japanese: "Wright's Imperial Hotel and its now famous floating foundations will go down in the annals of architecture with the Pyramids and the other great wonders of the world."

SULLIVAN: I'm glad now I wrote my essay. Maybe people will listen to me. *(Finished with the paper, he now tries to hand it to Lloyd)* Don't you want to read about it?

LLOYD: Later.

SULLIVAN: It is good for all of us. Are you all right? Anything wrong?

LLOYD: No.

SULLIVAN: Lloyd, give him credit. He was right, and you were wrong.

(No one knows what to say; they listen to the children.)

CATHERINE: They're having fun.

(Miriam slowly enters. She tries to "smile" and "be relaxed." The others, except for William and Sullivan, are surprised to see her.)

MIRIAM: Frank's still on the telephone. But now he wants to take a trip. What's the name of that beach?

CATHERINE: What beach? *(To Lloyd)* What is she doing here?

WILLIAM: I think you mean—Malibu.

MIRIAM: We'll take a picnic lunch, I thought.

WILLIAM: When does he want to go? I haven't prepared anything—

MIRIAM: And he wants to see some house.

SULLIVAN: The one in Pasadena.

KENNETH: That's in the opposite direction.

SULLIVAN: We'll go one way, and then the other.

CATHERINE *(To Lloyd)*: What is this?

(Lloyd too is confused.)

MIRIAM *(Looking at Kenneth)*: Hello. Have we met?

KENNETH: I don't think so.

(Kenneth looks at Catherine.)

CATHERINE *(After some hesitation)*: My husband, Kenneth. Miriam Noel. Father's—friend.

KENNETH: How do you do?

(They shake hands.)

MIRIAM: You're the banker.

KENNETH: That's right. Is it that obvious?

(Kenneth laughs at his joke, no one else does.)

MIRIAM: So I'm supposed to ask if we're all going on this picnic? That would be nice. *(To Catherine)* And how are you?

CATHERINE: We've met.

MIRIAM: I know. You have his granddaughter.

CATHERINE: That's right.

(Miriam suddenly smiles to herself.)

What?

MIRIAM *(Suddenly serious, trying to hide her smile)*: Nothing.
I was just remembering something Frank said about you.
(Looking off) Is one of those *("children")* yours?

CATHERINE: One is. Yes.

MIRIAM: Which one? Point her out. I'd like to know . . .

CATHERINE *(Hesitates, then)*: She's . . . You can't see her.

KENNETH *(Pointing)*: She's right—

CATHERINE: The blue dress.

*(Miriam looks off, says nothing. The others look off at
"Ann"; no one knows what to say.)*

Lloyd, you didn't know Miss Noel was here?

LLOYD: I didn't. Had I known I wouldn't be here.

MIRIAM: I like you, too.

CATHERINE: But, Miss Noel, I understand you'll soon be
going back east.

MIRIAM: Yes.

CATHERINE: That'll be nice. Won't it?

MIRIAM: We're talking about doing just that.

CATHERINE: We? *(She turns to Lloyd)*

SULLIVAN: Your father, Catherine— *(Catherine turns to
Sullivan)* —has asked Miriam to marry him.

(Pause. Sounds of the children playing.)

LLOYD: Catherine—

MIRIAM: I'm thinking about it.

CATHERINE: I don't understand.

MIRIAM: What's not to understand, Catherine?

CATHERINE: But Father isn't divorced from—

MIRIAM: In four weeks. It'll be final in four weeks.

LLOYD: No one told me this. Does Mother know?

MIRIAM: Why does she have to know? What business is it of hers? Is that coffee, Louie?

(He begins to pour her some coffee.)

SULLIVAN *(As he pours)*: Do you want something in it?

MIRIAM: No. No.

SULLIVAN: Good for you, Miriam. *(He pats her hand)*

CATHERINE: Kenneth—?

KENNETH: What do you want me to do??

LLOYD: Will there be—? I don't know what to say. Where's the wedding?

MIRIAM: I said—I am thinking about it. I haven't said yes. I want to be sure this is the right thing for both of us. *(She sips her coffee)* Chicago. We'll do it there. My friends are all there. We thought we'd go back with Louie. Have a party on the train. *(Smiles)* Like kids.

(Short pause, then:)

CATHERINE: That'll be nice.

MIRIAM: You'd be invited of course. You are his children. But I don't know if you want to come all the way to Chicago.

LLOYD: Probably not.

KENNETH *(To Catherine)*: If it's something you'd like to—

CATHERINE *(To Miriam)*: We can't. *(To Kenneth)* We can't leave Ann.

MIRIAM: Isn't it wonderful about your father's hotel? You know I never doubted him for an instant. It never even occurred to me to do that . . .

(Frank comes out. All turn to him. Awkward moment, then:)

CATHERINE *(Going up to Frank and kissing his cheek)*:
Congratulations . . .

FRANK: I'm sorry, I've been on the telephone. Everyone's
been—

LLOYD: I'm sure.

(From off, a telephone rings.)

FRANK: See? William—no more.

(William hurries off.)

(To Sullivan) He's happy. When the young are disappointed
in us—is there anything worse?

CATHERINE: I'm happy for you, too.

MIRIAM: Louie told them about you proposing.

CATHERINE: I didn't mean—! I wasn't congratulating—
I mean your hotel. I'm happy about *that*, that it didn't . . .

SULLIVAN *(To Frank)*: They brought the papers, have you
seen—?

FRANK: People have been reading them to me over the
telephone.

SULLIVAN: This one—they compare the hotel with . . .

*(He shows Frank the article. Pause as Frank reads. Miriam
tries to smile pleasantly. Sullivan pats her hand. Then:)*

FRANK: Lloyd, have you read this? *(Hands Lloyd the paper,
pointing out the article)* Read that.

(Lloyd "reads.")

CATHERINE *(Finally)*: So you are going back to Chicago to get
married?

FRANK: She hasn't accepted my proposal yet. Have you?

MIRIAM *(Teasing)*: And maybe I won't.

(She and Frank laugh.)

LLOYD: Jesus Christ.

FRANK: I think she's going to say yes.

(Miriam kisses Frank on the lips.)

Is that a "yes"?

MIRIAM: I told them about the picnic.

FRANK: What picnic?

MIRIAM: How we're all going on a picnic to that beach.

FRANK: Miriam wants us to go on a picnic. All I want to do is show Louie that house.

MIRIAM: We'll do that, too.

KENNETH *(To Frank)*: Would you be willing to—?

CATHERINE *(Interrupting)*: What? Why are you talking?

KENNETH: I was just wondering—I haven't mentioned this to Catherine—

CATHERINE: What?

KENNETH: If maybe you'd stop by our house—because of the addition? See how it— I understand you usually like to see the land before you come up with something. Lloyd told me that.

CATHERINE *(Trying to stop him)*: Kenneth—

FRANK: I do—like to see the land.

CATHERINE: I'm not sure this is the best time, Kenneth.

KENNETH: I don't understand.

CATHERINE *(Nods toward Miriam)*: I don't think it's the right time.

KENNETH *(To Frank, confused)*: Another time then.

FRANK: Just say when.

(Another awkward moment.)

MIRIAM: So we'll go to the beach.

FRANK *(His mind on other things)*: The Japanese ambassador himself telephoned me. He thanked me.

SULLIVAN: Good. Very good.

FRANK: Lloyd, the Japanese ambassador.

MIRIAM: So we will go on a picnic. To this beach. That'll be nice. It'll be good to get your father away from his work for a day. He needs that. He told me that last night. To think the worst has happened and then . . . it all turns out. We'll need to take two cars, won't we?

(No response, everyone looking at everyone else.)

So—who wants to ride with whom? Catherine and— what's your name?

CATHERINE: Kenneth.

MIRIAM: Thank you. Kenneth and—Lloyd? Do you want to go together? Or one of you drive with your father and us? You decide. *(No response)* We have room for one more. Lloyd?

(Lloyd and Catherine exchange a look; Miriam sees this.)

No one?

(Kenneth starts to volunteer, but is stopped by Catherine.)

Then it'll be you—and us. I should go and get a hat for this sun. Excuse me . . .

(Upset, she hurries off. Then as soon as she is out of sight:)

CATHERINE: I don't believe her. *(To Kenneth)* Now you see what I mean?

LLOYD: Does Mother know anything about this?

FRANK: This has nothing to do with your mother.

LLOYD: Goddamn it, Father, this is how you tell us?!

CATHERINE: Helen telephoned me last night, Father. After she stopped by to—thank you.

LLOYD: Why are you bringing that up now? Why are you saying it like that?

CATHERINE: Why do you think?

LLOYD: He didn't try and pick her up, did he?

(William hurries out and interrupts:)

WILLIAM: Mister Wright—Miss Noel, she asks if you could . . . *(Gestures "come inside")*

FRANK: What does she want? I can't.

SULLIVAN *(Head in his newspaper)*: Frank . . . *(Gestures that Frank should go to Miriam)*

WILLIAM *(To Frank)*: I don't know what to do, sir.

FRANK *(To Sullivan)*: I don't know why I have to—

SULLIVAN: Because she's upset. And you're marrying her. And she's going to take care of you.

FRANK: Why should I have to do this? *(He hurries off)*

CATHERINE *(Under her breath, to Lloyd)*: He's marrying that woman!

LLOYD: I heard! I have ears!

KENNETH *(To Catherine)*: Why don't I just drive with them?

CATHERINE: You don't understand anything. *(To Lloyd)* My heart's like this. *(Gestures pounding)*

(Kenneth has stepped away and now stands near Sullivan.)

SULLIVAN *(Still reading his paper; to Kenneth)*: This one is interesting . . .

(Off, Miriam cries out to Frank: "They hate me!" He in turn sh-shs her.
William starts to head inside.)

Stay out here. Anyone want some of the papers?

(No response.)

LLOYD *(To Catherine)*: He tried to pick up that girl?
CATHERINE: Look, there she is now. *(She waves off to Helen and "smiles")*
LLOYD: She told you he . . . ? *(He waves off and "smiles")* I don't believe this. He treats them all the same. Mother. This "Miriam." The same. I wish one of them would just hit him. *(He shouts toward the house)* Just hit him! Hit him!
CATHERINE *(Stopping him)*: Lloyd. *(He struggles with her)* Lloyd! Act your age. The children can hear you. Please.

(Lloyd calms down.)

It won't be any different than it's always been with him. Nothing's changed. Come here.

(He goes to her. She straightens his shirt and tie, brushes dust off his shoulder, smoothes back his hair. Then with a slap on the shoulder:)

We'll be fine.

(Frank comes out, this time wearing an admiral's hat and carrying a ukulele.)

FRANK: Miriam's taking a little nap.

(As he speaks, the others turn to him and notice his costume.)

CATHERINE: Father what are you—? *(To Lloyd)* What's he wearing?

FRANK *(Hesitantly)*: Remember this? *(Touches the hat)* Lloyd?

LLOYD: I haven't seen that for years.

FRANK: I brought it out here with me, to show the both of you. *(About the ukulele, to Kenneth)* I used to play this— when they were kids.

CATHERINE: At Christmastime.

FRANK: At Christmastime.

KENNETH: Why the hat?

CATHERINE: You'll see. *(Turns to Lloyd, excited)* I forgot about this, did you?

LLOYD: No. I didn't forget.

(Frank strums.)

Sh-sh.

FRANK: Sit. Sit.

(They sit and look up at their father with awe and love as he begins to strum and then sing, not very well:)

I am the very model of a modern Major-General,
I've information vegetable, animal and mineral—

SULLIVAN: I thought you hated everything English.

FRANK: Everything but this. I've always loved this.

SULLIVAN: You Welsh don't know how to hate. Not like us Irish.

FRANK *(Sings)*:
>   I know the kings of England, and I quote the fights
>   historical,
>   From Marathon to Waterloo, in order categorical;
>   I'm very well acquainted, too, with matters
>   mathematical—

CATHERINE: As you are!
FRANK: Thank you. *(Continues:)*

>   I understand equations, both the simple and
>   quadratical,
>   About binomial theorem I'm teeming with a lot o'
>   news—

(He pretends to search for the rhyme, others laugh, especially Lloyd and Catherine who have been transported back to childhood.)

I got it! *(Sings:)*

>   With many cheerful facts about the square of the
>   hypotenuse!

LLOYD AND CATHERINE *(Sing the refrain)*:
>   With many cheerful facts about the square of the
>   hypotenuse!

CATHERINE: Another one! Come on, Father.
LLOYD: And faster!

(Frank prepares himself, sets his balance, then:)

FRANK *(Sings)*:
> I know our mythic history, King Arthur's and Sir
> Caradoc's.

SULLIVAN: And I thought you were American!

FRANK *(Sings)*:
> I answer hard acrostics, I've a pretty taste for paradox,
> I quote in elegiacs all the crimes of Heliogabalus,
> In conics I can floor peculiarities parabolous,
> I can tell undoubted Raphaels from Gerard Dows and
> Zoffanies,
> I know the croaking chorus from the *The Frogs* of
> Aristophanes!
> Then I can hum a fugue of which I've heard the
> music's din afore,
> And whistle all the airs—

(He stops, nearly in tears.)

KENNETH *(Turns to Catherine)*: What's wrong?

(She turns to Kenneth, who sees that she too is crying.)

Why are you crying?

(Frank looks at Lloyd, goes to him and rubs his head as one does a little boy's. Then:)

FRANK: We should stop this.
KENNETH: Why?
FRANK: I don't feel like it anymore. *(He moves off to the side, in his own thoughts/memories)*
KENNETH *(To Catherine)*: What happened?

CATHERINE: It's how it used to be. I'd forgotten it. Let's go. I want to go home.

KENNETH: What about the picnic?

LLOYD: There isn't going to be a picnic today, Kenneth.

(Catherine hurries off, trying not to cry.)

KENNETH: I don't understand. *(He follows her off)*

SULLIVAN: I don't think I'm ever going to get to this Malibu.

WILLIAM: It's where you were the other day. It hasn't changed. I was making sandwiches. I'll put all that away.

(He starts to go, Frank stops him.)

FRANK: I don't want to go on a picnic.

WILLIAM: I'm putting it all away. *(He goes)*

(For a moment, Frank doesn't know what to do. There is an emptiness, then:)

SULLIVAN: I feel like drawing. Anyone else? Gentlemen? I'll bring out some sketchbooks.

(He goes off, inside.)

LLOYD: I'm surprised Catherine even remembers you singing that. She couldn't have been more than—five, maybe. The last time.

FRANK: She looked just like she did when she was small. Looking up like that.

LLOYD: Mother brought out the presents while you sang.

FRANK: I know. I know.

LLOYD: Ann—she looks just like Catherine did. The spitting image. You should spend some time with her.

FRANK: I will.

LLOYD: But it's not the same.

FRANK: No.

(Short pause.)

LLOYD: Congratulations on the hotel. I'm sure you are very proud of yourself. You always are.

(Frank looks at his son. Sullivan returns with the sketchbooks.)

SULLIVAN: Who wants to draw? I'll leave them on the chair.

FRANK: I'll draw.

SULLIVAN *(Sitting, opening a sketchbook)*: So why don't we ask Miss—the schoolteacher over, maybe she'd pose for us again.

LLOYD: I think she's busy. Maybe later.

SULLIVAN *(Sketching)*: Maybe later.

LLOYD: Father, would you like that?

FRANK: I don't do people.

(Lloyd has taken a sketchbook as well; the three now sketch. We hear the children playing, off. Sullivan sketches what he sees, off; Frank sketches what he is thinking, and Lloyd, again, begins drawing his father.)

Don't draw me, Lloyd.

(Lloyd ignores him and keeps drawing him. William comes out, hesitates, then:)

WILLIAM: Miss Noel—

FRANK *(Sketching)*: What William?

WILLIAM: She's asking for you.

FRANK *(Sketching)*: Tell her you couldn't find me.

WILLIAM: She saw you out . . . She knows you're— *(Stops himself and goes inside to tell her)*
FRANK: Louis, Lloyd's a better draftsman than both of us.
SULLIVAN: So you've said.
LLOYD *(Sketching)*: Thank you.

(Sullivan looks at what Frank is drawing.)

SULLIVAN: Your house in the desert?

(Frank nods.)

FRANK *(Looking at the ground plan he has just been drawing)*: Living room. With fireplace. Hallway. To the kitchen. *(Then imagines)* There's the kettle. The family around the table, waiting for their tea.

(Suddenly pleased with himself, he begins to whistle "I Am the Very Model of a Modern Major-General." Sullivan and Lloyd join in as they continue to sketch. All is quite jolly.)

(Sketching) Louis, I came out here to start again. Now— I'm going back. How did that happen?

(Frank stops, as if a cloud has crossed him. Sullivan notices this.)

SULLIVAN: Draw. Keep drawing.

(They draw.)

END OF PLAY

AUTHOR'S NOTE

Frank's Home is based upon a real incident in the life of Frank Lloyd Wright. I have attempted to stay true to the known facts, though I have consciously transgressed in two ways: Louis Sullivan was not in Los Angeles with Wright during this time (though his relationship with Wright is similar to as portrayed), and it took approximately ten days, not one, before Wright learned that his hotel had not collapsed. The following books proved especially helpful in researching the play: Meryle Secrest's *Frank Lloyd Wright*; Brendan Gill's *Many Masks*; Ada Louise Huxtable's *Frank Lloyd Wright*; Edgar Tafel's *About Wright*; Kathryn Smith's *Frank Lloyd Wright: Hollyhock House and Olive Hill*; Peter Blake's *Frank Lloyd Wright*; John Lloyd Wright's *My Father Who Is on Earth*; Frank Lloyd Wright's *An Autobiography*; Willard Connely's *Louis Sullivan*; Robert Twombly's *Louis Sullivan, His Life & Work*; J M Richards's *An Introduction to Modern Architecture*. Frank's speech in Scene 3, about building the Millard House in South Pasadena, is based upon a chapter from Wright's *An Autobiography*.

RICHARD NELSON's plays include *Farewell to the Theatre*, *Nikolai and the Others*, *Sweet and Sad*, *That Hopey Changey Thing*, *Conversations in Tusculum*, *How Shakespeare Won the West*, *Rodney's Wife*, *Franny's Way*, *Madame Melville*, *Goodnight Children Everywhere*, *The General from America*, *New England*, *Misha's Party* (with Alexander Gelman), *Columbus and the Discovery of Japan*, *Two Shakespearean Actors*, *Some Americans Abroad*, *Left*, *Life Sentences*, *Principia Scriptoriae*, *Between East and West* and *The Vienna Notes*. His adaptations/translations include *Tynan* (with Colin Chambers based upon *The Diaries of Kenneth Tynan*); Jean-Claude Carriere's *The Controversy*; Ibsen's *An Enemy of the People* and *The Wild Duck*; Molnar's *The Guardsman*; Strindberg's *Miss Julie* and *The Father*; Chekhov's *The Cherry Orchard*, *Three Sisters*, *The Seagull* and *The Wood Demon*; Pirandello's *Enrico IV*; Fo's *Accidental Death of an Anarchist*; Goldoni's *Il Campiello*; Beaumarchais's *The Marriage of Figaro* and Molière's *Don Juan*. He has written the musicals *Unfinished Piece for a Player Piano* (with Peter Golub), *Paradise Found* (with Ellen Fitzhugh and Jonathan Tunick), *James Joyce's The Dead* (with Shaun Davey), *My Life with Albertine* (with Ricky Ian Gordon), *Chess* (with Tim Rice, Benny Andersson, Björn Ulvaeus); the screenplays for the films *Hyde Park-on-Hudson* (Roger Michell, director) and *Ethan Frome* (John Madden, director); numerous radio plays for the BBC; and the book *Making Plays* (with David Jones).

He has received numerous awards both in America and abroad, including a Tony Award (Best Book of a Musical for *James Joyce's The Dead*) and an Olivier Award (Best Play for *Goodnight Children Everywhere*); Tony nominations (Best Play for *Two Shakespearean Actors*; Best Score [as co-lyricist] for *James Joyce's The Dead*); an Olivier nomination (Best Comedy for *Some Americans Abroad*); two Obies; a Lortel Award; a New York Drama Critics Circle Award; a Guggenheim Fellowship and a Lila Wallace-Reader's Digest Writers Award. He is the recipient of the PEN/Laura Pels Master Playwright Award, an Academy Award from the American Academy of Arts and Letters, and he is an Honorary Associate Artist of the Royal Shakespeare Company. He lives in upstate New York.